Shield IT Networks, Inc.
Santa Clarita, CA

ISBN: 9798342273121

Printed in the United States of America

Your Firm's Reputation & Future Are At Stake!

Steps YOU Can Take to Mitigate the Biggest Risks to Your Firm.

Scott Hagizadegan

Contents

Preface:

About the Author

Scott Hagizadegan is a speaker, entrepreneur, marine captain and philanthropist.

Prior to founding his current company, Shield IT Networks, Scott was the co-founder of Ignisis for over 20 years. He uses his 27 years of extensive experience with helping clients, who range from startups to Fortune 500s, including such well known clients in the financial and retail industries as Ernst & Young, FPA, Guitar Center, VF Corp, Vans, LAPD, 4 Wheel Parts, and Don Roberto Jewelers, with the design, implementation and maintenance of next generation networks.

Using a philosophy that design drives outcome, combined with his character and competence, Scott continues to earn high praise and trust with fierce client and team loyalty of over 6x's the industry average of 2.5 years, where his currently runs at 21+ years.

Scott is also very passionate about giving back via a hand up, not a hand out, and has led philanthropic projects raising funds and gathering teams to build computer labs at orphanages around the world (Zambia, U.S., Honduras, Dominican Republic, Mexico, etc.); is a volunteer leader at his daughter's AWANA class the past nine years; and has served on the Board of Retail Orphan Initiative – Zambia and currently serves on the board for Thrive In Joy helping kids in the U.S. and abroad,. He continues this deeply held belief in his business life via a "Profit with Purpose" approach that simply means we earn profit with the purpose of reinvesting it into the needs of the world around us as a "Serving Leader".

His favorite hobby is adventuring the islands and waters off the coast of California on his yacht *Andiamo* with his family, friends and clients. As a licensed Captain, he also operates one of the top chartering businesses in Southern California.

You can connect with Scott at:
scotth@shielditnetworks.com | 818-489-9877 | ShieldITNetworks.com

Chapter 1:

Have You Already Been Hacked?

Every 11 seconds (5.5 in CA, double national avg) a cyberattack occurs.

The global cost of cyberattacks has now reached the trillions. The business world is a different place now, and quite frankly, if you want to succeed, cyber security needs to be at the forefront of your business strategy.

So, is your company prepared? Maybe a better question is, how sure are you that your company hasn't already been attacked.

In this chapter, we're going to talk about how your firm might already be hacked. I'm going to cover three surprisingly easy ways that any firm can tell if you have a security breach and what you can do about it.

First off, you're probably wondering, who the heck is Scott Hagizadegan and what does he know about protecting my firm? Well, it all started when I was very young, and my family had to flee our home country. My father brought us to the United States with nothing, and had to start all over. Both my mother and my father worked two jobs just to put food on the table. They eventually started three different businesses over the next several years.

The problem was that each one of those businesses failed. I saw the devastation it had on my father, and how it personally impacted him. My father gave his business everything he had to build it from scratch. Of course, these failures also took a financial toll on the family. I have to admit, though, what really stuck with me was how every time he got knocked back down, my father got back up and would do it all over again. In reflecting on that, I think that's what planted the entrepreneurial seeds within me to someday take the risk to start my own business and, like my father, start from scratch. Just as many of you have.

Unfortunately, I've seen firsthand the devastation that a ransomware attack can have on businesses and firms. As entrepreneurs, it's in our blood to "dodge bullets", as I like to say. You're battling headwinds from the economy, recession, COVID, global closures, challenges with your clients, and accounts receivable and payable. You adapt and you learn how to duck and weave. However, when a cyber incident happens to a firm, it's truly devastating.

I observed one such incident happen to a firm I was brought into recently. They had heard about the work I had done with other firms, but their situation was different. I got to see firsthand the impact it had on the lives of everybody on the team at this firm. I saw the fear they had about whether the organization was going to continue and when their next paycheck was going to come. I helped the partners go through the challenges with the breach, with their sensitive client data, and with the conversations that needed to happen with their clients as they tried their best to recover. It's a very fearful and dark situation. You really learn a lot about what truly matters when you're alongside a firm that's going through that.

That's why I've ultimately made it my mission to protect the livelihoods of millions of employees, as well as the entrepreneurs that took all the risks to start these organizations. I put the emphasis on the employees because, to me, people matter most.

Seeing the devastation that the hackers can cause gives you firsthand experience that everything is about prevention in our industry. As Benjamin Franklin said, an ounce of prevention is worth a pound of cure; but in the world of Cyber Security, an ounce of prevention is worth a *ton* of cure. Let's start off by exploring two conflicting truths and ideas here. First of all, while it's a very dangerous time for your firm to be online, it's also an absolute must. There's some important things for you to know to protect yourself; your business requires it.

Here's some industry stats that we've gotten from numerous internet crime reports. In 2020, 65% of organizations had their email compromised *(Internet Crime Complaint Center, 2022)*. In fact, Business Email

Compromise was found to be one of the biggest threats to firms. The number is just going up from there, from what we've seen. In fact, in 2021, that number increased, jumping from 65% to 77% of organizations that had a Business Email Compromised *(Internet Crime Complaint Center, 2022)*. Like I said, Business Email Compromise is one of the biggest threats to your business. Now, consider the fact that you probably sent 30 emails yesterday. Your emails may have tricked some people into giving sensitive data, such as somebody else's social security numbers.

Hackers running an email compromise sit and view the communication. When they get into your email, they're able to watch everything and tailor the attack specifically to how you communicate with each other. It's all based on the trust that you have with your vendors, with your clients, and with your peers they interact with. When hackers are in your email and they're able to view that information, they can then be very specific in their tactics.

This reminds me of the story of one firm that we were brought in to help. Unfortunately, we were brought in after the fact. This organization's CEO was very big on philanthropy; he had a huge heart. Everybody in his organization knew he loved philanthropy, and he'd occasionally send them emails regarding his philanthropic work. So when his email was compromised, the hackers caught wind of how he spoke to his executive team and the type of things he'd support. Based on this, at a time when they found out that he's going to be traveling, the hackers sent an email to the company's CFO, acting to be the CEO. The email said that he really loved what a particular organization was doing, and that he wanted the CFO to go ahead and send them $75,000. The request and verbiage were typical of the CEO at this firm, so the CFO sent the money. It wasn't until the CFO and CEO spoke later on that they discovered the CEO never made this request, and the money was gone. That's one example of many of the types of things that we see. This really talks to the sophistication of the email compromises.

That means you have two problems when it comes to your email. First, the personal information within your email is likely a treasure trove waiting to be infiltrated by hackers. Second, the risk of being caught is so small. In fact, in 2022, out of 2.8 million attacks and breaches, only one individual was arrested. High rewards and low risks means more money per success. This happens because vulnerabilities keep popping up over and over. In fact, 2022 was a record year for vulnerabilities *(Expel, Security Operations, 2023)*.

Here's some context to help define vulnerability. Ask yourself this: In your car, what are the vulnerabilities? Are the windows rolled up? Are the doors locked? Is the alarm set? Now, let me give you an example that's not so obvious. Between 2015 and 2019, Kia Automobiles were twice as likely to be stolen. There was a missing anti-theft feature that would verify that the key belonged to the person who owned the car. This anti-theft feature is something you assume they would have, right? When the bad guys got wise to this, they pounced on the opportunity. It was a simple oversight, but one that the bad guys definitely knew about. The average driver didn't know, though.

While this example helps us to understand the definition of vulnerability, the number of ways a hacker can get into your computer are exponentially higher than the ways they can break into a Kia. According to the Cybersecurity and Infrastructure Security Agency (CISA), 2022 was a record year for vulnerabilities, with a staggering 26,448 reported *(CISA. gov, 2023)*. That is a staggering number. Of these 26,448 vulnerabilities, 59% of them could be used to break into your computer systems and steal all of your sensitive data. This is far more valuable than a Kia. Furthermore, more successful attacks continue to occur, which means more money out the window.

Hacking is a big business. In 2019 alone, cyber security breaches have cost businesses over $2 Trillion *(University of North Georgia, 2024)*. A lot of executives don't really understand the frequency of these security breaches, so they think it won't happen to them. They assume that hackers are just going after the big guys. However, that's not what the industry stats and the FBI analysis shows.

Try to imagine what a 2 Trillion Dollars worth of security breaches would look like. Picture holding $10,000 in hundred dollar bills in your hand. This would be just a small stack in your palm. Take that stack up to $1,000,000, and you're looking at about a pizza box size of hundred dollar bills. Next, $100 Million. This would be about the size of a crate. A Billion dollars would look like 10 crates. Two Trillion dollars would look like two entire stacks of crates. That's how much money Hackers made in 2019 just through security breaches.

These costs to organizations are crippling, and it's projected that by 2025, the 2 Trillion Dollar loss in 2019 is going to jump to a staggering $10.5 Trillion *(Cybercrime Magazine, 2020)*. To put that in perspective, $10.5 Trillion is just under the two top economies in the world: the United States and China. If Security Breaches were their own country and economy, they would come in as the third biggest economy in the world.

It's pretty clear that hacking is a big business. Here's how you can identify if you're already a victim. After all, studies have found that three out of four organizations were at risk of being a victim to hacking *(Statista, 2024)*. There are a lot of folks that have already become victims, and some may not realize it.

You may already have an IT Person or IT Team, which may make you think that this isn't your job. However, if and when there's a breach, who's going to communicate to your top clients about what happened? Ultimately, that's what's going to matter when it happens. Also, security quickly becomes your number one priority once that happens, because it brings everything to a screeching halt. Furthermore, the reality of it is, you're going to be negotiating with the criminals. There are even companies whose sole purpose is to negotiate with the criminals on behalf of business owners once you get hit with ransomware. Ransomware is such a big problem, it's created an industry of its own.

Ultimately, it's you that's going to be dealing with the repercussions of the security breach. As the main stakeholder, you need to verify that these things are not happening to you and your organization, because you're the one that's going to be cleaning up the mess and dealing with the follow-up. You might think that having cyber insurance will take care of things if anything happens; however, it doesn't matter if you have cyber insurance. It's certainly good to have cyber insurance, but this is something that you do not want to go through to begin with. While cyber insurance is a good safety net, remember, an ounce of prevention is worth a ton of cure.

Here's an example. You may have auto insurance, but you also understand how much trouble an accident can cause. When an accident happens, time slows down, right? Your progress stops and your focus completely changes. What can you do? Simple: be prepared. To prevent an accident from happening in the first place, you drive carefully. You take the proper precautions to lessen your chances of being involved in an accident. The same idea applies to cyber security. The best thing you can do is simple: be prepared.

When was the last time you had a third-party audit done to verify that your team, or whomever you've outsourced to, are securing your network properly? We're rated top 5% in cybersecurity in the United States, and I still have our team and our network perform third-party audits every three months (quarterly). As a firm you shouldn't audit your own work. Nobody can do it alone. Vulnerability assessments take out the mystery so you can have peace of mind knowing that everything is being done correctly, or you can proactively tackle the vulnerabilities.

Let's explore how to know if you are already a victim to a security breach. First, we're going to jump through some of the telltale signs that indicate that something bad is already happening on your device. Next, we'll go through your network and talk about how the breach is spread.

Unfortunately, that's always what happens. Research conducted by IBM found that hackers are in an organization's system for an average of 197 days before they are even detected. Once detected, it takes another 69 days to contain the attack *(IBM, Cost of Data Breach Report, 2023)*. This is usually because once they land, hackers spread throughout your network before they lock everything down and you get the dreaded notification that everything's been hacked. Lastly, like we touched on, we're going to go over some telltale signs that your email has already been compromised and some things you can do to jump on it earlier, which is key.

Let's start with your device. There are some telltale signs that will indicate something bad is happening on your device. One of the most common signs is if your device is running slower than usual. By that I mean you open applications that you usually use and they take a long time to open or refresh. The apps just keep spooling and spooling. Oftentimes, you'll begin to hear loud noises coming from your computer. These noises are due to the fans running longer than usual.

Additionally, your device might start to overheat. That's another good indicator that you may want to pause and bring it to your IT team's attention to have something looked at. Another sign may be random programs popping up out of nowhere, which looks like a bunch of windows flashing by really quickly. That's a telltale sign that something's not right. Next, updates will stop working, and you'll be unable to open files that you were previously able to open. By the time it's too late. The last step is the obvious: the ransom note. After those 197 days, they've locked everything down, and your computer and entire network's been hacked.

Now, let's go over how to figure out if your network has been hacked. How do you know if somebody's already gone beyond your individual computer? For one thing, passwords unexpectedly change. You attempt to log into websites that you have previously logged into regularly, and they ask you to re-enter your login information. Also, you encounter a slowdown, but this time it's the internet. Pages are taking a lot longer to download.

You also might start getting reports from other organizations, such as clients or vendors, that say that they're receiving emails from you that you don't recall sending. The last and final thing (again, when it's too late) is when you get a knock at the door and it's the FBI. Obviously, you've already been hacked by the time they are on to it.

I was working with this firm that we helped go through a breach. What was really devastating was not only did their network and operations come to a screeching halt for roughly 45 days while they did not have access, but they also had to deal with paying the bad guys. Then, to add insult to injury, they had to settle three different lawsuits with three different district attorneys in three different states, even though they were a company out of California. It turned out that some of their clients whose information was breached resided in other states. That component alone cost them $1.9 million.

Business Email Compromise *(BEC)* is a major problem, resulting in $2.7 Billion in losses annually. That is an astounding 79 times more than the annual losses due to ransomware *(FBI Internet Crime Report, 2022)*. One telltale sign that your email has been compromised is that you start getting crazy amounts of spam. This is a good indicator that something's going on. Attackers like to create a smoke screen, which is why you're seeing so many emails. You're so distracted with having to look at all the emails coming through, meanwhile the hackers can go in and manipulate, delete, and redirect emails.

Sometimes business email compromise involves an update to your signature. We see that a lot in firms when their email is compromised. The attacker sends out a message and the receiver calls you back on the phone number. Then, the hacker is able to actually intercept the call.

Other common tactics include the hacker creating new forwarding rules, to enable wiring money to the wrong account. If you notice that your email is alerting you that the new forwarding rules have been created, that's a definite time to bring it to your team's attention.

Another red flag may be finding emails in your sent items that you don't recognize. This one's interesting. If the bad guys are worth their salt at all, they will usually go in and delete emails they send with your account so that you don't catch them. However, if you get communication from anybody that they received an email you don't recall sending, you may want to check your sent folder and your deleted folder to see if there's anything there. When people are complaining that you're sending them strange messages, that's an indication that the attackers might have access to your contacts and are trying to target them. What they'll do is they'll take an executable file, put it in an email, and send it out to everybody. If your clients and vendors think they're getting an email from your firm, they are more likely to open the email and click on links or attachments. In these types of attacks, hackers leverage trust. Trust is the common ingredient in these types of things and why they're so damaging beyond just your company. These situations cause embarrassment and pain because they spread to the people closest to you.

With all this in mind, what can you do? You might still be thinking that this is just a concern for your tech team. I'm going to share the stat that really alarmed me. A recent study found that of the 3,000 companies that were hit with ransomware over 18 months, all had one thing in common: 100% of them had firewalls and antivirus *(John Merchantson, Blackpoint)*. Unfortunately, many people think firewalls and antivirus are sufficient, but what you did yesterday is not good enough for today. Security, specifically cybersecurity, is a constantly moving target. As I said before, having antivirus, a firewall, a tech team, and backups will not protect you or your organization. Usually, when they get into your network, your backups are deleted as well.

So how do you know if your network is secure and working properly? That's the million-dollar question, right? Ultimately, there's always going to be blind spots. Nobody can do this alone. As I mentioned before, we even have our own networks audited every third month by an independent third party.

This third party analyzes our cybersecurity, costing me roughly $8,000 per analysis. I usually purchase packs of 10 at a time for our clients, and right now I have three left that I have available to use. I'm offering my final three executive cybersecurity risk assessments worth $8,000 each to the first three people to reach out. Fully complementary, all you have to do is go to our website, **csoscott.com**, and secure one of your three licenses.

You might be thinking, "I'm not the right person" or "I'm pretty sure I'm protected". Again, like I said, when there's an event, aren't you going to be the person that's going to have to deal with the fallout? Are you completely protected? One of the biggest things you're going to get from this assessment, which is a huge value, is this: peace of mind knowing your network is protected. You were verified via a third-party audit. 9 out of 10 insurance policies now require you to have an assessment done at least once per year, or they will cancel your policy or increase your rates by 200–300 percent. The assessment will give you the peace of mind that you've done everything in your power to protect yourself, your employees, your clients, and your reputation.

Our third-party's assessment tool is one of the best in the industry, and one of the highlights is that no admin credentials are obtained, therefore maintaining the integrity of your network. Just like the bad guys would do it, most penetration tools will ask you for your admin credentials. The third party we use does not request these credentials, setting it apart from other assessment penetration tools. Secondly, most penetration tools usually have you install programs or other things on your network, which is not the best practice. We don't install anything on your network with the third-party assessment tool that we use. We begin by having your entire security and system analyzed. Then I will meet with you to go over the results, where you'll learn the simple steps that you can take to protect yourself.

The executive summary is of major value. It puts everything in high, medium, and low-risk vulnerabilities, if we find any, and then it gives you the remediation steps of what you need to do. Perhaps you'll get a clean bill of health and be able to sleep well at night knowing that you're protected properly. Peace of mind is ultimately the goal for all of us, right?

You're probably wondering then, what's the catch? Again, there's no catch to what we're doing here. I'm doing this to protect one million individuals and firms from becoming the next ransomware victim. What if you're not ready for the assessment? Like I said, I only have three and I know the timing may not line up for you. Even at $8,000, I have to tell you, it's worth its weight in gold.

I'm going to give you some easy ways to tell on your own whether your security is working properly. I spent some time pulling together five simple signs that you have weak cybersecurity. If you're interested in that, we have a copy of the article "Five Simple Ways You Can Know If You Have Weak Cybersecurity" *(Groff Networks, 2023)*. Go to **csoscott.com/5signs** and grab your own free download. Just take a read through it to understand your possible risk exposure.

Chapter 2:

Avoid a Reputation Ending, Crazy Expensive Compliance Nightmare

This very important chapter is going to go over five simple steps that every CEO can take to avoid a reputation-ending cybersecurity incident and a very expensive compliance nightmare.

Those steps include recognizing cyber security is an issue that requires your attention, knowing the rules and regulations in place, designating a specific person as the cyber security expert on your team, understanding the "why" behind your compliance policies, and remembering less is more. This chapter will also address how your firm might already be hacked, three surprisingly easy ways any firm can determine if they've had a breach, and what you can do about it.

The first step every CEO can take to avoid a cybersecurity incident is focusing on compliance. First of all, I have to make sure that you know that compliance is, quite frankly, a nightmare. There's no way to put that nicely. That's because compliance requirements are often put together by various organizations. When it comes to compliance, there is so much to consider, and some of it may go against the organizational culture that most businesses have in place.

These requirements or regulations can be very difficult. What I mean by this is that the policies that come out of these requirements can be really hard. Some of the requirements are hard to enforce and are ultimately hard to understand. Furthermore, there's so much to consider. For example, let's break down the latest FTC safeguards rule. This one alone has 168 different subsections that are involved with the requirements. That's 5,000 words. It breaks down into nine individual key major elements. Besides that, there are an additional 30 minor subsections.

A key point when talking about compliance is that daily culture eats compliance for breakfast every day. Every morning compliance even gets up, our daily culture runs into this problem because one of the key things is that compliance is not fun. You get busy with everything you have in your day-to-day business and then some corners get cut. Ultimately, a bad habit starts to develop. Make no mistake, though; this is really important because compliance does matter.

There's a difference between compliance and security. The problem is, in today's environment your firm needs to worry about both. There's a major divide between what compliance is and what security is. Ultimately, even though you might be compliant, it's not going to mean that your firm is secure. However, both are equally critical and important.

So, what is compliance? Compliance is meeting specific standards and protecting your clients while responding. Sometimes you have to respond only after there's an event. On the other hand, when it comes to security, the focus is on keeping your organization safe and responding to a threat when something happens. Both, though, are about keeping an organization out of trouble.

So, what happens if you are not compliant? Well, no one is going to come knocking at your door. This is not how regulations work. They're not going to do an audit in your environment and find out if you're compliant. You're probably thinking that if nobody's going to be looking, you're not going to get caught. That's not quite how it works, unfortunately. When you have an event such as a ransomware attack, and you're knocked down and the most vulnerable, that's when the investigators are going to come in and look over every one of your configurations. They're going to look at every inch of your setup and see what you did wrong.

The problem is, when you have a breach, these auditors are not going to see you as a victim. They're not going to see you as the person who was just breached and was devastated by this. They're going to see you as the person that's responsible for the breach. You're guilty of negligence until you've proven otherwise. Not only will you have to overcome this awful event, dealing with the ransomware or a data breach, but you're going to have to deal with the fines and all the violations that come with it. With the new FTC regulations, you have fines up to $1.5 million. There's even language in there for up to five years in prison. It gets very expensive. Note that these are individual fines. In most cases, multiple offenses are found.

So what do compliance and security come down to? There are two contributors. One is human nature. It's human nature to underestimate future risk. We're all wired this way. The second is culture. There's a couple of components here. The first one is simple. Nobody likes to be told to follow the rules.

If you don't believe me, here's an example. Let's say that you were driving to work today, and someone with you noticed that you were speeding. How would it make you feel if this person pointed it out to you? Going a step further, have you ever had one of the blue and red lights flashing up in your mirror? Have you ever had somebody pull you over because you were speeding? When this happens, you're hoping the police officer won't give you a ticket. And have you ever gotten that ticket? Even though you've gotten that speeding ticket, do you still speed? Think about that. When it comes down to compliance, speeding is as simple as it gets. It's a requirement that's three words long. Speed limit, 65. You see these words on your way to work multiple times in a day. Yet, we all still speed, and we still get pulled over even though we knew that was the rule.

So, how do you prevent this from happening? How do you keep people breaking the rules within your company? Having consequences and then breaking the rules again? What's crucial here is that we have to change the way people think.

There are three misconceptions about compliance that we should explore. The three most common misconceptions are that cyber security is just an IT issue, or that they already have someone who handles the security, so they don't need to worry about the rules. You shouldn't assume that compliance is an IT issue. Security is everyone's responsibility. Some other common misconceptions include not needing to know the "why" behind compliance, and the less is more approach. It's important to understand the "why" behind compliance policies in order to fully comply. There are three compliance areas that this chapter will cover: the physical aspect, the technical aspect, and the administrative aspect. IT only covers the technical aspect. Essentially, compliance is just a piece of your security program.

Where does compliance fit into this? We have three things: compliance, technology, and security. What's the difference between these three things? Technology is about getting something done as quickly and as cost effectively as possible. Whereas compliance, on the other hand, is about following and adhering to a set of standards. Security is about protecting the organization from risks.

Let me give an example of what we're talking about. If we think about it from a technology standpoint, we need to come up with a solution to get where we're going. Technology is about getting something done as quickly as possible and as cost effectively as possible, so we invest in the automobile. However, now we have a new problem. Not everyone is making it to their destination. So, what can be done about this to get there safely?

In 1901, the very first speed limit was introduced. Shortly after speed limits were put into place, safety for the passengers riding within automobiles also became a priority. In 1959, the very first seat belts were introduced. However, there was a problem. Nobody wore them and not everyone had them.

That's where compliance came into play. Compliance is about following the standard. The solution was simple: add seat belts to cars and then require that people use them. However, there was still a problem: nobody wore them. It wasn't until 1984 that seatbelt legislation began to be passed by the states. Now, people were required to wear their seatbelts.

Let's say you're driving along under the speed limit and wearing your seatbelt. You have everything lined up. You're fully compliant. But are you secure? What if your car was to catch fire spontaneously? Would you be safe? That's where security comes in. It's about keeping you from the risks. So, on the security side of things, we want to consider all the risks that come with travel and make sure we address them. Security is about protecting you from risks. This is why it's not just an IT issue.

Let's take a look at the rules next. What do you know about the rules? Why do you care about these rules? I still remember the worst speeding ticket I ever received. I was going 20+ mph over the speed limit. I was pretty scared because I knew at that point, my car could be impounded as well. I have to tell you; the police officer was not sympathetic when I explained that I didn't know what the posted speed limit was in that area. It did not matter one single bit. I'd fallen into a speed trap.

In the example above, although I may not have known the rule (the speed limit), I still received a speeding ticket. That's how it goes for compliance. It's the same exact reality. It's really critical that everybody in the organization, especially the leadership, understand what the rules are that you're responsible for.

Next, let's talk about why you may want to have a specific person responsible for this. Culture is about changing the way people think. Getting people to change what they think isn't just about writing rules. It's not that simple. It's about trying to enforce the rules, and what you need to do is come up with a way to turn people's heads.

One key way is having a champion on your team to make this change. This is one of the best ways to communicate the why behind the compliance components. This person will help make sure other people in the organization are on board. Now, picking the right person is absolutely crucial, and finding that person can be difficult. Ultimately, there's someone on your team who always complains and is always pointing out issues. When you talk about having somebody who's passionate for compliance, they're most likely going to volunteer. Don't pick them. You do not want that individual being the one in charge of this.

Let's get into why these rules exist. Remember, there's a big difference between being compliant and being secure. How do we make sure these rules are being followed? Making sure both compliance and security go in the same direction is a big challenge. Knowing the spirit of the standards helps you address both. Security posture and compliance can be simultaneously improved if you understand what the standard is looking for and why it's going into place.

If you think about the speed limit and the seatbelt analogy we've been discussing, driving was very dangerous before standards were put in place. Then, after the standards were put in place, people started coming up with ways to follow the standards, which led to much greater safety and fewer injuries from accidents. It's the same for cybersecurity.

Let's look at some cybersecurity statistics. According to a recent study, 80% of US organizations have already been breached in some way *(Trend Micro's Bi-Annual Cyber Risk Index Report, 2021)*. That means they've experienced the breach or they've already experienced ransomware. On average, a hacker is inside your network for 197 days without you knowing it and before the big lockdown happens on a network and they ask for the ransom. I think you would agree that those numbers I just shared with you are pretty shocking. That's why we're starting to see more and more standards going into place around compliance when it comes to security.

Next, let's talk about how to get started. You see a lot of folks want to get everything going at once. They want to get everything moving in their security and compliance. That's a bad idea. Don't try to boil the sea. Instead, what you want to do is pick the individual spots where you're going to have the biggest gains and impact. Then, move the ball forward.

How you do that is by performing an assessment. You know, one of my favorite quotes comes from Peter Drucker, a management guru over the last 40 years. Simply, he would state, "Once the facts are clear, the decisions jump out at you". What you want to do is get an assessment to figure out what is currently working on your network, that way you can figure out where your gaps are. Identify these gaps inside your organization and figure out what's missing. That's when the decisions will jump out at you on what you need to do.

Once the assessment has been completed, prioritize the work that needs to be done. One of the most critical pieces of the whole puzzle here is documenting your decisions as you go. This is key for compliance.

You're probably wondering where the heck do I start? How do I get started on this? If this is something that you want to do, go to **csoscott.com/analysis** and secure your free level one risk assessment that we'll perform to get you all the facts on where your security is lacking. These assessments, if you go out anywhere, start at $8,000 and go up to $30,000. I'm offering these assessments to you completely complimentary. If that's something that you want to do, again, go to **csoscott.com/analysis** and make sure you secure your free analysis. We're going to analyze your risks, and the information obtained is extremely high in value.

By the time we are done, you'll receive an executive summary that breaks down the results into high, medium, and low risk vulnerabilities that we found on your specific network. It'll show you specifically what we found, and it'll give you the remediation steps that either you and your team can tackle, or you could bring it to us for us to do it for you.

Like I said earlier, this assessment tool will help you create your action plan. This gives you a detailed roadmap. There's no catch here, in case you're wondering. As I said at the beginning of this presentation, my deepest mission and goal is to protect the livelihoods of 1 million people. It's as simple as that. If this is something you want to do, make sure you get a roadmap on what you need to do to get your firm secure. Begin by understanding where you're at today and create a roadmap from there. Go to **csoscott.com/analysis** to get your free level one risk assessment.

Chapter 3:

Are Your Employees Helping Hackers?

You may not see it, but your employees may inadvertently be helping hackers.

In this chapter, we'll go over seven common employee habits that you need to put a stop to immediately. Those habits include faulty or weak passwords, mishandling sensitive information, disabling security tools, opening infected emails, using personal devices at work, using public or free-wifi, and playing the victim. I hope that this section gives you a handful of nuggets that you can take back to your team and make a meaningful impact on improving your security posture. Remember, prevention is everything.

More than 90% of all cyber-attacks begin with a phishing email *(CISA. gov, 2024)*. That's all it takes. Imagine learning that somebody on your team let the hacker in. 95% of all breaches involve an employee mistake *(Terranova Security, 2023)*. Human error leads to more data breaches than anything else. What kind of human error causes this, you might ask? How are attackers using human error to get into your firm's network? Most importantly, how can you defend your organization? How can you keep your employees from screwing up and letting a hacker into your network?

The answer is simple: you need to know how people become victims of cybercrime and what mistakes allow attackers to get in. The first mistake I'm going to go over in this chapter are errors made with passwords. This is probably one of the most important. Think about how you identify yourself on a computer. You log on to show that you're the actual person that's allowed to control your computer and gain access to it. Hackers impersonate users all the time, and once they get your passwords, they have all the time in the world to get to everything else. 61% of cybercrime involves compromised credentials *(Verizon Data Breach Investigations Report, 2023)*. They use a password to get in and impersonate someone on your network.

You may be wondering how this happens. There are a number of habits that your team has that make this possible. One of them is never changing passwords. This is human nature. Do you enjoy changing your password? Probably not; none of us do. You and your team members might use simple passwords or maybe reuse passwords because it's too difficult to memorize 70 different passwords. Another common pitfall is using a pattern to come up with a password. For instance, if you use welcome2021!, the hacker will suspect a pattern. That's exactly how many people fall victim to cybercrime.

Another example of a bad habit that your employees might have is storing these passwords in vulnerable places, like Word documents or Excel spreadsheets. Hackers know about this habit. Best practice would be to consider some type of password manager. Storing passwords for you within a secure network, having a password manager is one of the most cost-effective and easiest things you can do to improve your security.

You're also going to want to talk to your team about passwords, and the importance of creating a strong password. Sit them down and go over some of the things in this chapter. Furthermore, don't forget to search the dark web. Many of your passwords may have already been breached, and they could be for sale for pennies on the dollar without you being aware.

Now, let's go over mishandling sensitive information. People on your team may be making your firm less secure by mishandling the most important information. Let me give you an example of what we're talking about here. Have you ever downloaded your tax files? Where did that file end up? Are you putting documents like that into your Downloads folder? Maybe you're uploading it to your cloud storage like OneDrive, Dropbox, or Google Drive? Maybe you're just saving it onto your desktop? Maybe you put it into your Documents folder? These places are the first places that the hacker is going to look because it is such a common habit among employees. Therefore, hackers are going to find passwords and other sensitive information very easily.

One easy step to combat this problem is to have your employees add password locks to any documents or files that contain sensitive data. While this may not completely prevent the bad actors from getting access to it, it's going to make it a lot more difficult and take them much more time. Then, it turns hacking into a time game. How much time does the hacker have on your device? This is where the advanced tools that we implement for firms really come into play, catching threats proactively before they're able to spread to the rest of your network.

Another thing you should do is make sure that all of your computers are encrypted and your company has policies in place surrounding the handling and storing of data. You'd be shocked how often this simple step is overlooked. Think about the sensitive data you keep, and all the things that you might have downloaded in the last six months. There's a setting on your computer where you can go in and simply encrypt the file and prevent this sort of oversight from happening. Make a point of talking to your team about how they handle sensitive data. Make sure that they do not send these files via email. Do not store them on just normal cloud storage. Verify that your team is using approved cloud storage.

Next, let's dive into disabling security tools. I know what you're thinking: nobody on my team would ever disable the security tools on their device. But have you ever felt like your computer was running slow and you wanted to speed it up quickly? Maybe you had a deadline for an important project. Maybe you had a file that you just couldn't open because the security tools were blocking it. Maybe there was a website that you couldn't get to because your firewall was mistakenly preventing you from getting access. You and your employees may turn off security tools all the time just to open a file. Sometimes, people connect to their cell phone to get around the corporate firewall to get work done. Also, have you ever turned off your backups to get your device to run faster? Have you ever been in such a hurry that you didn't allow your computer to get updates? Do you ever really have time for security patches? These are things that we see all the time, and some of the habits attackers expect you to have.

Furthermore, you and your employees might be ignoring the messages that indicate that something is wrong when they come up. As an example, think about warning messages in your car. There is the check engine light that pops up right in front of you. So what do you do when you see that? You immediately have a mechanic check it out to make sure it's not something major. But what if that showed up on the right-hand side of your radio display, real small?

This is what happens on your computer. The area where a warning would appear is not in front of your eyes. It's actually way off into the corner where it's often overlooked. All the time, we see situations where employees have no idea that a very important message is coming up.

What you can do about these things is evaluate the security tool configurations that you have. Evaluate the devices to make sure they're getting updates. Finally, look at your antivirus. Make sure it's not locked down in such a way that allows your employees to go in and disable it if they want, or at least that you get alerted if and when they do.

Now, let's get into opening phishing emails. With AI, it's gotten substantially even more targeted. Studies have shown that More than 90% of all cyber attacks begin with a phishing email, and 65% of all hackers use spear phishing as their main method to gain access to a network" *(CISA.gov, 2024)*. Again, what's happening is a lot of folks are ignoring the signs.

There are a number of signs that every single phishing email has, and it may come from an unfamiliar email address or an email address that looks legitimate. One key indicator is if there is a sense of urgency. Also, it may have a generic greeting or salutation; something you're not used to seeing from that person. There might be some spelling or grammar mistakes in the email. Sometimes they have suspicious links. This can be a major red flag that you need to keep your eyes peeled for. Any single one of these items is enough to bring everything down. That's not even the entire list of everything that's potentially available.

Other risky behaviors we're seeing are employees opening attachments. Your security tools don't stand a chance if one of these files gets opened. So what can you do about it? Let's dive into some possible solutions.

Make sure that anti-phishing techniques have been implemented in your operation. Educate your team on what each type of file means. Consider testing the users with simulated phishing attempts. That's a crucial step to educating them over time.

Also, make sure to consider what devices you and your team are using. Do your employees use their own smartphones for business email? We see this all the time. Do you know how those phones are protected? Is there any software on there to verify? Do you know if your employees or phones are getting their updates on there as they're supposed to? You may not know this, but most phones stop getting updates from the manufacturer once they become three years old, so ask if any of your employees are using phones that are over three years old for work. Also, consider encryption. If your phone or your employees' phones are lost or stolen, hackers are going to get access to your data. We see this all the time as well.

Furthermore, think about authentication. Are they using complex pin numbers or just the standard three to four pins? Really think about that for a minute. You can actually break into a phone in just an hour or less and have access to everything on that device. Recently, hackers have begun stealing people's phones to get access to their PIN that gives them access to all your company's sensitive data.

Imagine for a second that you're putting in that four-digit pin on your bike lock and there's somebody looking over your shoulder, memorizing your pin. What they do next is access your settings and they lock you out. Then they can access any accounts with phone access. Then they block you completely out of your phone.

What can you do about it? One simple step is to require a complex password to access your email. You can also have encryption requirements, so the device actually has to be encrypted in order to store any company data on it. Again, talk to your employees about smartphone theft where the attackers take physical possession of their phones and steal their pins. Make sure people on your team understand why it's important to protect their smartphones as well when they use it for work.

Along with phones comes public Wi-Fi. There are a lot of folks out there that are going to end up using public Wi-Fi. Would you ever consider yelling your username or password across a busy coffee shop to someone? Heck no! Somebody could be listening in, right? That's the problem with public Wi-Fi. Hackers and other people on the network can hear everything that's going on between your computer and the different services that you're getting access to while you're there.

Worse, hackers create fake wireless networks that look like the real thing and then they're going to know where to find people like you. They're very targeted and smart about who they go after. They know what to name these networks so that your devices can even automatically connect to them. Then they perform eavesdropping. This is where what's called the "man-in-the-middle" attacks come into play.

When you go to something like a website and the server sends a website over, you need credentials. It sends you a multi-factor authentication request. Then you log in using your MFA code. That's how you gain valid access. Now imagine if there was somebody in the middle. There are tools for this that you can even download off the internet and build out these evil websites that look exactly like the original website. Basically what's happening is you're going to the fake website and not realizing it and they're getting all of your data.

Imagine going to a coffee shop and you hop on the Wi-Fi and then go to your bank's website, but it's actually a fake site that looks just like your real bank website. Then, the site tells you that it looks like you were connecting from a new location, so it asks you a few questions to validate your identity. Very standard, right? Would you do it? This is exactly how these man-in-the-middle attacks work.

Once connected, your employee decides if they're going to trust the other devices on the network. On most public Wi-Fi, because it's public, your computer can see all the other computers on the network. With one simple click, that employee can make all of those other devices talk to their computer.

Make sure that every employee uses their smartphone tether or uses a smartphone as a wireless connection so they're not using public Wi-Fi. Talk to them about the dangers of connecting to these public Wi-Fi hotspots. Implement an always-on VPN connection to make sure it's securely done.

The last habit is the most dangerous one that we're going over in this chapter. It's called playing the victim. Essentially, this involves thinking that there's nothing that can be done. The hacker is going to get in anyways. You might think that security is not your job, or that your IT has always kept you safe, but this will not always be the case. When somebody on your team bypasses their security tools, there's nothing that the IT team can do. This is why it's important to not put it all on IT's shoulders.

What can you do about this? First, talk to your team about participating and protecting your data and how important it is for your organization. Make sure that you're going through and talking to your team about limiting their privileges. Lastly and most importantly, get a risk assessment. Of course, FTC safeguards have made it mandatory for you to do so.

Chapter 4:

The Dirty Little Secret That's Making It Easy For Hackers To Target You...And What You Can Do About It!

In this chapter, we're going to target the dirty little secrets that hackers are using to target firms and just a few things you can do today to reduce your risk exposure.

First of all, you need to know that the average ransomware demand is only going up every year. To be specific, ransomware attacks increased by 84% in 2023 alone *(NCC Group, 2024)*. To put it in perspective for you, in 2019, the average ransomware for a business was only about $84,000 *(Coveware, 2020)*. Remember, this was pre-COVID. In the last three years, the latest data puts the average ransomware demand for a business at $5.3 million *(IBM, 2023)*. That's $5.3 million on average. That means, as a business owner, you're going to be down a minimum of 15 days before you're able to be up and functioning again. Sadly, studies have also shown that due to these cyber attacks, 60% of small businesses actually go out of business within six months of an incident *(National Cyber Security Alliance)*. The ones that have insurance and enough resources can bounce back, but it hurts no matter how you look at it. Basically, it's all about prevention.

Imagine if your firm was hit with ransomware when you came in this morning. You come in like every other day and you log in to your system. When you log in, you realize that none of your files are working. In fact, your desktop files look a little bit funny. When you try to log into something like QuickBooks or Microsoft Excel, they're showing as offline as well. You don't realize what's happening yet, but things are running super slow.

Now, you've probably done this before when the internet has been down. You begin using offline forms. However, this time, you find that something's a little bit different. You attempt to log into your computer, and first it says, "Server not available". Then, when you are finally able to log in, none of your files are working. Word, PowerPoint, or Excel simply won't open. Things are not adding up. That's when you find a file that says "readme.txt".

This is what it's like when you have an event. How can this happen, you might ask? Your firm does all the right things. You've invested in all the security tools. You've been paying for security services. You even have somebody who's responsible for your computers. In fact, your computer person seems brilliant. They always bail you out when something goes wrong. You have the right people. When there's a problem, you go to them and they fix it for you. Simple as that. You've even put a compliance program in place. Last month, your firm received an award for how well your compliance program was running. In addition, you also have the latest next-generation 24/7 security monitoring tools. So how could this still happen?

Bottom line, there's a dirty little secret nobody's told you about. Cyber security tools alone cannot keep you safe. Do you think that 50% of firms that fell victim to ransomware last year were all negligent? Do you think they weren't doing the right things? Do you think they weren't spending good money on all the security tools like we mentioned? They believed that they were fully safe and didn't have to worry about events like this.

Recently, our security team got pulled into an event. The firm in question had invested in all the right things. We're talking advanced antivirus, smart firewalls, intrusion detection, and even multi-factor authentication. They even had advanced tools like application control and off-site backups. They had next-generation 24/7 security monitoring.

Before I go through and explain what happened, let's dive into that real quick and take a closer look at these security tools. First of all, this firm had advanced antivirus. When the bad guys break in, it should go off. It should also alert the police and your security team.

Now let's discuss the smart firewall. A firewall is like a baggage scanner at US Customs when you're at the airport. It scans both directions in and out. Anything that goes in or out of your firm is scanned without the scanner slowing down the process. This way you don't have to wait an hour to get through the line like you might at LAX or San Francisco. You're able to open the luggage with a special key to see what's in it. It's not only looking for weapons, but other items that your firm might have, like confident client information.

The next one is a very important one: intrusion detection and prevention. Imagine you're on a deserted island, but you don't have anything to protect your camp. One way to protect your camp would be to dig a big hole and cover it up with leaves. If somebody attempts to walk up to your camp, they may fall into the hole. That's intrusion detection. With intrusion detection, you can see if they've disturbed the leaves, and they won't be as likely to continue looking around your island.

Then you have your multi-factor authentication. Basically, when you want to access things in your system, the system has to make sure that you are who you say you are. How that works is you first enter your username, then your password, then you have to provide one more thing. This can be a fingerprint or a simple code on your phone or physical device.

Next, we're going to jump into application control. It only allows specific apps to run in your environment. Basically, even though you might download or run an application, it might not be able to do certain things. It's like using your credit card. Even though you can swipe it, it might not work if you didn't alert your bank that you were traveling.

One of the other things this specific firm had in place was image-based off-site backup. This particular type of backup is helpful because it allows you to restore your system very quickly. Remember way back in the day when you rented VHS tapes, and how you could play the movie and make a copy of it at the same time? All you needed was another VHS player. This is how image-based off-site backups work. You can play them back on any computer and get up and running as quickly as possible.

The next thing they had was actually one of the most advanced next-generation technologies: 24/7 security monitoring. Remember the alarm system that we talked about? If you had the alarm system and didn't pay for a monitoring solution, no one would call the police, right? Same goes for your security program. If you don't want to just alert the user, you probably want the police involved. That's where the rubber meets the road.

Now, let's circle back to the firm I mentioned earlier who believed they had all the right systems and protections in place. They received an alert around 9pm on a Friday night. The bad guys most commonly attack when it's off after hours, usually over the weekend. The initial yellow flag was that there was strange traffic coming out of their network. The security team then began their response. However, the hackers were already ahead of the game, as is usually the case. By the time the security team recognized there was strange traffic coming out of their network, the hackers had already attacked 48 stations and broken into nine servers.

But how did they get in? Why didn't the security tools that we just covered that they had in place protect them? This all comes down to the simplest of mistakes that impact computers: human error. That's right. The attack wasn't because a user clicked on a link. This wasn't a phishing attempt. The attackers were successful because of a change in the configuration.

Let's go back to the smart firewall that we talked about in their security stack. It's inspecting all the traffic coming in and out of your organization. Remember, think of it like a scanner at US Customs when you're at the airport. Everything gets inspected as it comes in or goes out. Now, what if a big line starts to form and the personnel start a new line that doesn't go through the scanner? Instead, a security agent waves everyone through. No matter how good the security was for the other line, the bad guy would still have gotten through.

Basically, this is what happened to the firm. One of the people who had supported their computer systems simply created a way for an attacker to bypass their smart firewall. They bypassed the security scan. The bad guys got in and the organization was no longer safe with one simple mistake.

How do you prevent these types of mistakes, you ask? What you need to ask is, why did this happen. We've analyzed hundreds of networks within the span of a year, and this is more common than you expect. These things happen because of Cognitive Bias, a systematic thought process caused by the tendency of the human brain to simplify information processing through a filter of personal experiences and preferences *(Gillis, TechTarget, 2023)*. Think about your computer support team making changes to your infrastructure. They add new services, connect new vendors, replace devices, create new users, and change out products all day long. While they do this, security tools often get in the way. Due to Cognitive Bias, they may choose to bypass these security tools temporarily, thinking they have enough IT knowledge to still keep the organization and system safe. However, that may not always be the case, and this leaves a back door open for hackers to get in.

Let me give you an example. You're unloading your groceries from your car while your car is parked in the driveway. You live in a super safe neighborhood. Would you leave your trunk open while you unload everything? This is where cognitive bias comes in. People feel like their computers are in a safe neighborhood. The truth is that their computers live in a virtual, war-ravaged apocalyptic wasteland. Crooks and thieves are on every corner.

Your neighborhood feels safe because you know the people who live there. There's even a little bit of accountability. Your computer, on the other hand, is a different story. With your computer, everyone has access to the internet. Ultimately, everyone is right around the corner from you, including the crooks and thieves. Going back to the "unloading your car" example, what if somebody called you in the middle of unloading your car? What if they called to tell you there was an emergency and your dad was just taken to the hospital? You would probably drop everything and call him, forgetting about the open car. This is what happens to people in IT every single day.

There are always emergencies. They always plan to come back and close the car, but that might not happen for some time. This is all the time the hackers need.

So, what can you do? Inspect what you can expect. Are your security tools actually working? Run advanced antivirus checks to make sure that you have the proper tools running. What is the easiest way to do this? Is there a way to do that via script? Check to see that you have a smart firewall protecting you.

Last, you need intrusion detection, an absolute essential component of your firewall. Is it currently active and working properly? Make sure you have MFA on your most critical business applications. At the minimum ensure you have MFA on your banking, computer files, client data, and any off-site backups. Did you know, monthly testing of the restoration capabilities of your back up system is best practice and essential? You'd be shocked how often an incident happens and a firm believes they had backups, only to find out that it was corrupt and/or they weren't restored regularly.

What if I could give you an easy way to check a few of these? To automate it so you can quickly get a snapshot of what's working? Here's an example. If you were to look at the bottom right corner of your computer next to the clock, there should be a blue shield. That's for your antivirus. If it's up and running, you'll be able to quickly see a green checkmark. If there are any issues and for any reason it wasn't able to run or be updated, you wouldn't see this. Also, if you haven't ever been blocked when you've tried to visit a site, then your firewall probably has not been set up. What about MFA for your cloud services and bank accounts? Do you have MFA set up for both?

Next, let's discuss backups. Try the following experiment. Copy (don't move) an important file to your computer's desktop, then add the words "backup test" and today's date to the file content. I want you to leave it in there for 24 hours and then delete it. Now wait three days and contact your IT person and ask for it back. What you're trying to find out is how long does it take to get restored. Does the new file have your updated text in it? Sometimes they'll pull up a previous, older version. That's why I want you to change the name, so you could verify the one they successfully restored was the one you deleted from your desktop. Then you'll get peace of mind that your backups are being done effectively.

The easiest way to do all this, if you don't want to go through this manually, is to get a third-party cybersecurity analysis. In fact, with the FTC safeguards regulations in effect now, you're required to get one once per year.

Are you still wondering if you're the right person? Here's the simple answer: when or if there is an event, will you be the person that has to deal with the fallout? Are you going to be the person that has to talk to all your clients and let them know what happened? Based on the knowledge you've gained this far, do you think you may not be completely protected? Is it possible that not everything is locked down and secure? If the answer is "yes" to any of the questions above, you are the right person.

Chapter 5:

Recognizing and Addressing Insider Threats

This chapter is going to cover insider threats and how would you know if somebody inside your firm is actually working with the hackers.

You know, we focus so much on all of our security tools and the outside threats. Meanwhile, a lot more often than you realize, things happen from the inside, whether it's intentional or mistakes.

The frequency of attacks is extremely alarming. According to the latest studies, cyber breaches happen once every 11 seconds in the United States (CyberSecurity Ventures, 2023). To put it in perspective, cyber security breaches happen as often as car accidents do in the United States. In fact, in California, the rate of cyber breaches is double the rate of car accidents, with a breach occurring once every five and a half seconds (IC3 Report, 2022). What may be even more astonishing is that the average ransomware demand for businesses is 5.3 Million. Comparatively, in 2019 the average ransomware demand was only $84,0000. The number only continues to increase every year.

We've all heard the stories. The bookkeeper has a hard time making their rent one month. They decide to pay themselves just a little bit extra that month. Nobody notices. Nobody sees anything different. The following month, maybe they decide that they're going to pay themselves just a little bit more. They tell themselves that they deserve it. They actually think to themselves that they should be making more money anyways for what they're doing right now. They see thousands of dollars going out the door to vendors; on the payroll they see other people that are making more money than they are; and they decide to pay themselves just a little bit more. They don't even see it as theft. They justify the entire thing in their head. Sometimes they think that they'll pay this back anyways next week or next month. They think that nobody is going to be wiser, if they just borrow money for a little while.

This goes on for years, and tens of thousands becomes hundreds of thousands of dollars. By this point, there's no way they're ever going to be able to pay it back. Eventually, the person retires. Ultimately, the new bookkeeper starts and starts to notice some discrepancies, and they bring it to your attention.

You go through it with them, and you point out that it couldn't be so, because that person was so nice. They seemed to be fully committed to the firm and you just wouldn't expect anything like this from them. When the truth all comes out, this person actually ends up going to jail. So their life is ultimately ruined as a result of this. To top it off, your firm never sees a single penny of the money that they stole. It's a lose-lose situation for everyone involved.

I'm here to tell you that this could have been avoided. Research shows that 34% of organizations are affected by insider threats annually *(Sisa Information Security, 2020)*. That's why it's so popular and always seems to happen when people aren't paying attention. In fact, insider threats have increased 47% between 2018 and 2020 *(Ponemon Institute, 2022)*. The recession, high inflation, and increases in the cost of living are likely part of the reason.

Imagine you get a notice that the federal payroll taxes haven't been submitted for over 90 days and you get a notice that you owe some money. In fact, you owe a lot of money. One of your employees reports that they had an issue reporting their taxes to the IRS. A few days later you learn that another employee was told that somebody submitted a tax return already on their behalf. Then, you start learning about fraudulent unemployment claims that were popping up for your firm. That's when you realize that something is not right. A few weeks later, you get a strange call from the IRS, who have some questions for you. Many of your employees have fraudulent tax returns submitted on their behalf and the IRS believes that it's related to your firm. After weeks, it's uncovered that your HR person shared their password to the payroll system. Then, about a month goes by and they quietly quit working for your firm.

The investigation persists, and the IRS has some more questions. Now local law enforcement has gotten involved, and you learn that your HR person received $35,000 in cash to provide access to your payroll system and now they're long gone. So the local news crew shows up doing a story about crooks and the effects of being scammed and you decide that maybe this is an opportunity for some free publicity. Maybe your story is going to help some others. They do an interview, ask you some questions, and when the story comes out, somehow you're no longer the victim. They've pointed to you as being negligent. The damage is done. I've seen it all.

Insider threats typically start with two things. The first is access to your assets, and the second thing is the reason for the crime. What I'm talking about is availability and motive. It's actually more like availability and excuse, because ultimately the insider threat uses excuses to justify their behavior. It's not as much a motive as it is justification for why they are doing this. For example, "Why shouldn't I get more?". Often, they perceive some sort of wrongdoing by their firm, and use this as the justification for their poor decisions.

Most firms have tremendous risks associated with insider threats, and they're not prepared. What causes insider threats? Here are some startling facts for us to look at. Studies found that 79% of IT leaders believe that employees have put company data at risk accidentally in the last 12 months; 61% believe that they have done so maliciously; 30% of IT leaders believe that data is being leaked to harm the organization; lastly, 28% believe that employees leak data for financial gain *(Help Net Security, 2019)*. Some causes of data breaches include employees stealing data, employees intending harm, and lack of proper training.

Ultimately, does it really matter if it was malicious or intentional? The results are the same. The worst part is that when the story breaks, you won't be portrayed as the helpless victim. Instead, your firm will be labeled as negligent and irresponsible.

Then the FTC will show up to try to figure out what you did wrong. Unlike criminal law, where you're considered innocent until proven guilty, you're going to have to prove that you're doing the right things to be compliant with the FTC Safeguards, all because of a simple insider threat. This problem is even substantially magnified with the newest FTC safeguards. You're going to have some very high fines that are tied with it.

Now, let's go over five steps that every firm can take to reduce the firm insider threats. The first one has to do with new hires. Call and screen employee's references. Most firms just don't take the time to pick up the phone and talk to somebody about the person that they're about to hire, like past employers. Find out how that individual performed and why they left. If you find the previous employer or reference is very limited in the information they're providing, I like to ask "Would you bring them back on your team?". If nothing else, confirm the dates they claimed to have worked for that firm.

Another important step is to perform background checks. Although background checks give us a wealth of information, did you know that background checks only go back five years? Because of this, you should Google the individual. Start with a wide search. After you search their name, if nothing comes up, put their home state, then maybe their home city. Look for any articles that come up about them that might guide your decision.

Next, let's talk about hunting disgruntled employees. This is an important one also because these are the folks that become your biggest insider threat. Disgruntled employees are pretty easy to spot. First, they stop participating. Maybe they stop attending the extra functions that your firm does. You might also see a reduction in collaboration, or all you may see they stop working with other people on the team all together. Maybe they stop trying to engage with others in the organization as much as they used to. You'll also notice a lack of motivation. Maybe they slow down the work. Maybe somebody that used to be a superstar is no longer acting that way. You also might notice an uptick in them calling in sick. Maybe they become absent from work or they may come in late more often than they used to. Finally, you might see a decrease in performance. These are all key indicators that the person is disgruntled. Pay close attention to these folks. Why? Ultimately, when it comes down to it, these are the folks who are intentionally or unintentionally letting attackers into your network.

Now, let's dig into security training. Make sure that you're offering regular security training to your entire team. You're probably wondering why security training is important. For one thing, sometimes strong employees still make mistakes. However, training them on the right things to do, even if they're not fully engaged, does reduce the chances that they're going to make those mistakes that will make you vulnerable.

Training also helps enforce the behaviors that you want at your firm. More importantly, it teaches them what to look for, such as when that disgruntled employee makes that mistake. It helps them see the risky behaviors. It also increases the chances that they say something when someone is doing something improperly.

The fifth step you can take to reduce your firm's risk of an insider threat is secure off-boarding. Secure off-boarding involves having a documented checklist which goes through every single step when somebody leaves your organization. Don't wait until your first employee leaves to test the process. Go through and test it first. In addition, when somebody gives you notice, I suggest removing them from your firm as soon as possible. Consider eliminating their access and paying them for the last two weeks immediately, whenever possible. Make sure all accounts are turned off. Also make sure to check that the individual is completely disabled from your key financial resources and software applications they use at your firm. Often inside a firm, email and personal devices are overlooked during an off-boarding, but these are things you want to look at very closely. On the email side, you may have somebody on your team want to go through and monitor their emails and messages for the next few days or weeks.

Now, let's talk about evaluating your cybersecurity. Your most important defense against insider threats is, ultimately, your security program. Most security programs and firms focus on external threats, as I previously mentioned. They focus on how to keep the bad guys and hackers out of your environment, not thinking about the very people inside the environment and on their team helping the hackers to get their data. I want you to focus on both. If a hacker gets your employee to click on a link, then they abuse their privileges, they're officially an insider threat, right?

So, where do you start? The easiest and most effective way to do this inside of a firm is to start with one simple step: eliminating trust. What I mean by eliminating trust is going through and creating the "least privilege". Least privilege means only giving people in your organization the amount of trust they need to perform their job. This helps with external and internal threats, so you get a double benefit.

There are a couple of key factors here. The first one is, a lot of times when people think of least privilege, they're only thinking about data. I want you to go one step further and think about access. The last thing I want to mention here is avoiding permission creep. Avoiding permission creep is important. Permission creep is when somebody moves from one position to another, but maintains their previous position's permissions. When they get a raise and maybe move on to a management role, do they still need the old permissions they had previously? Ultimately, their permissions follow them from space to space. This results in folks inside your organization who have been there for a long time and started working as perhaps a staff assistant, they've moved up to manager, and then maybe up to partner at some point. Now they have access trails that go back years.

So where do you start? The easiest way to do this is to have a third-party analysis.

Chapter 6:

3 Warning Signs Your Firm Has A Cybersecurity Crisis

In this chapter, I'm going to go through several warning signs that your firm might already have a cybersecurity crisis.

I will also cover ways to identify whether or not you have a cybersecurity crisis.

I want you to imagine for a minute that everything you're doing is right and correct. You've invested thousands of dollars in cybersecurity, and you've built out a complete compliance program for the FTC. You've even provided cybersecurity training for your entire team. Additionally, you have a cyber insurance policy as a safety net. You've done everything in your power to make sure your firm and all the clients' personal information is safe. Even after doing all of that, is your network actually safe from hackers?

Unfortunately, it's probably not. Let's go over the numbers. According to a 2019 Google Study, 6.8 million accountants get hacked every day and 158 accounts are compromised actually every second *(WCNC, 2021)*. Now, do you think that all these people are irresponsible? No, they've invested in security tools just like you have. Then why were they still getting hacked?

The simple answer is that it's usually a problem with human error. Organizations are often wasting money on cyber security and protecting the wrong things. The worst part is, they don't even realize it. The reason for that is people are missing the warning signs. I'm going to cover the top three warning signs that indicate your firm has weak cybersecurity, including a bonus indicator you've never thought of. These are simple warning signs that anybody can recognize. You don't have to be a technical whiz. We won't be coding them in geek speak. I'm going to go over each one of these with you in plain English. Hopefully, you can use this knowledge to improve your security posture.

In a study of 6,000 networks scanned over the past 12 months, several common warning signs were present. Why aren't these warnings picked out sooner? Nobody wants to ask questions, create more work, and assume that something is wrong. It's just more comfortable to assume your security is taken care of. Note that we're not talking about compliance here. Compliance is a whole different thing. Every firm needs to wrestle with compliance to meet the FTC safeguards, but that doesn't necessarily mean that they're all secure.

We're going to go over just some simple warning signs that indicate your firm has weak cybersecurity. The first warning sign is if you've ever experienced a breach. The next sign we're going to talk about is if you have a lack of an incident response plan. Then, the final sign is that you assume that your security is already handled properly.

How do you know if you have had a ransomware event already? It goes something along these lines. First, you notice that you can't access some of your files. Someone in your firm may start complaining that they can't access some key data. Eventually, every computer in your firm becomes inaccessible. Lastly, you receive a note asking for payment to regain access to your systems.

Now, in more sophisticated attacks, hackers will steal your data from your firm and then send a note threatening you with blackmail. They're basically working on that desire to keep your data breach a secret. Ultimately, that becomes their weapon. If any of this sounds familiar, you've probably experienced a ransomware event.

What about email compromises? As I mentioned in previous chapters, business email compromise is one of the most common forms of cyber security breach. Has anybody in your firm ever had an email compromised? How would you know? It's pretty straightforward:

- Has anyone ever impersonated someone on your team by sending an email as them?

- Has anyone at your firm ever had confidential info accessed in their email?

- Has anybody in your firm ever been asked to wire money to the wrong person?
- Has anyone ever asked you to buy gift cards for them?

These are all signs of email compromise. Even if you didn't wire the money or pay the ransom, these events indicate that there's something going on. Something's wrong. Attackers are getting past your defenses. They're getting in your computer files.

The most important piece here is that the research shows 38% of victimized organizations will actually experience a repeat ransomware attack *(Barracuda International Survey, 2023)*. This happens because hackers often leave what's called a "backdoor". A backdoor is where hackers leave a way to get back into their victims' networks, even if you've paid the ransom. These are often easy to create and nearly impossible to find.

So, if you ever had a compromise, you're going to need to update your security program and introduce new controls. Think of it like protecting a castle. If your enemies got past the front gates and inside the court, they probably left a rope behind to get back over the wall. Even if you find and remove the rope, they still know how the castle security works, since they were already inside the castle. They know how all the defenses are set up and they've seen all your weaknesses. In a data breach situation, when attackers break into an email system, they often install a simple tool that lets them back in without even having a password. Therefore, if you've experienced a breach, you need to change the methods you're using to protect your data.

Next, let's talk about a lack of an incident response plan. What is exactly an incident response plan, and why is it so important? Do you remember back when you were in elementary school and you had a teacher who would tell you what to do if there was a fire? They basically walked you through what you needed to do as a kid if you saw or experienced a fire. They would tell you exactly the steps to do, like yell fire and check to see if the door is hot. Your class would go through every single step in a very detailed manner. You don't want to wait for the fire and then expect everybody to know what to do. You create a plan, communicate it, and plan for it. This is a common and best practice.

Here's the startling statistic: you're five times more likely to experience ransomware or a data breach than a fire, and 67% more likely to experience a cyber attack than a physical theft *(Aviva, 2023)*. That's the simple truth of it. Wouldn't you prepare for a ransomware attack or a data breach just the same way? Yet many organizations aren't prepared, which ends up being devastating. This is one of the key requirements of the FTC regulations. Our team does this all the time with firms. We help them develop incident response plans.

Let's go over what should be included in a well-prepared incident response plan. The very first thing you should include is a section on prevention. I can't emphasize this enough. An ounce of prevention is worth a ton of cure in cybersecurity.

You will also need to know things like how to train users. Additionally, you're going to have a section on detection, which explains how to report suspicious activity. What are you looking for when it comes to cybersecurity? And if you notice something, who would you tell?

In addition to training, we're going to need to set up some sort of containment. This is about preventing the spread of the incident by keeping the attackers from getting into other resources in your organization. Once you've laid out a plan for containing the attack, you're going to need a section on eradication. What steps is your organization going to take to get the hacker out of your environment?

You're going to need a section on recovery. This section is really about taking action so that your firm can resume normal sales operations. You'll also need a section on notification, which means going through and notifying the individuals who will be impacted by the data breach of the ransomware breach.

Finally, you need to include notes for using what happens during an incident to improve the plan. This is a very simple framework for building out an incident response plan, as well as each of the sections that should be included.

Maybe you've already got a plan in place; but how do you know that plan is an effective one? Just like planning for a fire, you're going to want to communicate, review, and test your plan. So think about it:

- Have you reviewed your cybersecurity incident response plan in the last 12 months?

- Have you actually gone through and analyzed the plan to make sure that it has the right sections that we just covered?

- Are you prepared for the three most common types of cyber events (ransomware, email compromise, and data breach)? Do you have a section in your plan for each of these?

If you have reviewed it, have you actually practiced it? This is often called a tabletop exercise. It's a chance to go through and exercise your plan and make sure everybody on your team knows exactly what to do.

Now, let's go over the last and probably the most important mistake: assuming that you already have cybersecurity handled. The sad thing is, out of the 1683 vulnerability assessments we've done with our security team over the last 18 months, 92% have found major vulnerabilities. And guess what? The majority of them had IT staff or MSPs that they used. I don't want you to walk away from this thinking that they're not doing their job right. That's not it at all. The fact is, in cybersecurity, nobody can do it alone.

All we do is cybersecurity for firms, and yet we don't do things alone. We're one of the top 5% rated in the United States, but we still have third parties that audit our team every three months. Don't exempt your team as part of the leadership. It's essential that you don't expect your IT team or your MSPs to do it alone. Using a doctor analogy, an MSP is like going to your general practitioner or your family doctor for routine stuff. A general MSP maintains your networks. A lot of them also do cybersecurity in addition to that, but they're not hyper-focused on it. Using the doctor analogy again, if you have something that requires specialized care, you would go to a specialist. That's who we are—we are your specialist in cybersecurity.

That's why it's essential to have a third party that specializes in auditing. You've probably heard somebody say, you need a culture of security. What do they mean by that exactly? Well, for a cybersecurity program to be effective, you need the entire team to be on board, especially the leadership. Think about physical security for a minute. If one of your employees leaves the front door to the office unlocked, clients' private data or other information and documents could be stolen out of the filing cabinets overnight. If one of your other employees noticed it, they would point out the problem, right?

You need to have that same sort of behavior when it comes to cybersecurity. If one of your employees is taking a risk that allows hackers into your firm, someone should be prepared to point it out. You might get ransomware, or hackers might steal all your information. You would then have to go through and communicate that to all your clients. The problem with most firms is that the employees are not looking for weak cybersecurity the way they do with physical security. It's a silent killer, if you will. This is why it's so critical to have a culture of security on your team. Start discussing cybersecurity with your team and your organization. You can go into the importance of building out a cybersecurity program. Work as a team to create your plan.

Now, as I mentioned earlier in the chapter, I'm going to give you a bonus at the end. You see, we analyze a number of firms, as I mentioned already, and they often don't realize the true value of their data. They also didn't have proper security controls around that data. Therefore, take the following quiz to find out if you're properly securing your firm's data. Answer each question with a "yes" or "no":

1. Do you protect all types of data at your firm with the same amount of effort?

2. Do you have different protocols protecting remote workers than those that are working inside the office?

3. Do you store data in the cloud like Google Drive, Dropbox or OneDrive?

4. Do you use multi-factor authentication when it comes to accessing email?

5. Do you ever receive simulated phishing training? This is when somebody sends you a fake email that simulates a hacker trying to get you to click on something, etc.

6. Do you receive phishing emails from time to time from your team?

7. Do you ever receive cybersecurity training for the team? This is specifically about being trained on things like an incident response plan. For example, for our firms, we have a one to two minute video sent out weekly that is entertaining and at the end it asks four questions. By sending out these short videos and quizzes weekly, we're able to slowly educate their staff. Again, nobody can do it alone, so this is crucial to have. Do not expect your IT guy to do it alone. It helps create that culture, and it's also one of the key parts of the new FTC regulations.

8. Do you ever email personal information, social security numbers, date of birth, or any other information about your clients that could help pick them out of a group of less than 10,000 people? This could also be for receiving emails from clients. We know that a lot of firms have low-tech clients that will email this type of sensitive data. Has that been addressed in your firm?

9. Do you ever store passwords in Excel, Word, Outlook, or on your smartphone?

10. Do you use passwords that are longer than eight characters, that include uppercase, lowercase, special characters, etc.?

11. Do you ever reuse the same passwords or a pattern to your passwords so that somebody could basically look at one or two of your passwords and guess what the other passwords might be?

Go through the quiz and review this information with your team.

Chapter 7:

Preparing For A Cyberattack

This chapter will cover preparing for a cyber attack and how to rebuild your firm without sacrificing your reputation.

I'll also get into why the next move is so critical when an incident happens. You must acknowledge how important this topic is in cyber security, and what a huge threat it is, as most business owners don't realize it's the single biggest threat to your operation and has the power to bring everything to a screeching halt. The FBI stats are pretty staggering on the frequency of attacks on small firms. Most firm operators are not aware that according to the FBI, a firm gets crippled with ransomware every 11 seconds *(CyberSecurity Ventures, 2023)*. Putting it plainly, that's the same as frequency car accidents in the United States. For those of you that operate firms in California, the rate of ransomware is one attack every 5.5 seconds, which is double the rate of car accidents *(IC3 Report, 2022)*.

As you know, there's been a major uptick in cyberattacks. This began with the COVID closures, and continued to worsen during the Russia-Ukraine war. Since then, nothing has slowed it down, it just continues skyrocketing. Recently, our security team was working with the victim of one of these attacks. I got a chance to speak to their CEO while we were working on the forensic side of things and trying to get them back online. He mentioned that, at one point, he would have paid anything to get back online and get his operation back up. So why was he in this situation to begin with?

First of all, it's because they weren't prepared and didn't have a plan for what they would do next. Best case scenario, this recovery was going to take over a month to get everything back up and running. I won't sugarcoat that fact. Things like their backups were destroyed in this situation, as is often the case. If that happens inside of your organization, you have few options. You need to think through what the next steps are going to be. Option one, of course, is to pay the hackers and get your data back. The second option is to use a six month or even a six-year-old copy of the data that was backed up when you were doing a project.

Meanwhile, you're losing your clients' trust. This is a major problem. People are calling into your firm and expecting computers to be working. More importantly, they're expecting you to know what's going on. In this particular case, the CEO actually sent out an email to all of his clients saying that their computers were all offline. You're probably thinking that's silly. Why would they do that? Imagine being in that situation. Imagine putting together that email that's notifying your clients that something's going on in the heat of the battle. All while you're tired and trying to deal with not being able to access your computers. Could you just imagine the frustration? Would you make the right moves if you were in that same situation? What would your communication to your clients be like if that were to happen tomorrow?

In this chapter, we're going to cover five simple things that you can do to make sure that you don't end up in this spot. First, we'll talk about making a plan, and how to properly document your plan. Next, we'll go over a strategy around disclosure. Then, we'll talk about who should be on your team. Finally, I'll list who you should call when this happens.

Let's dig into making your plan. It's not surprising that having a plan helps, but how much does it help? A firm with a written recovery plan in place can recover from a cyber attack in an average of 20 days. On the other hand, a firm that doesn't have a plan can take an average of 71 days to recover. What's surprising, then, is that over 77% of businesses do not have a cybersecurity incident response plan *(Ponemon 2019)*.

Why is this happening? Some people are just too busy. Others might be worried that if they put the plan together, things might change, making their original plans obsolete. Many people might be thinking that it's never going to happen to them. However, as I mentioned previously, the stats starkly show the opposite. Some people think that their IT guy always figures these things out, so there's no need to worry about it. Despite this, it's worth the investment. How much is a plan like this worth? Think about it: 71-20=51 days. How much work can your firm get done in 51 days? How many new sales is that? Obviously as a firm, if it's tax season, 51 days could be crippling to your operation. How much money would you lose during those 51 days while you attempt to recover? All because you didn't have an effective incident plan in place.

You need a plan, then you're ready to start the process. Always start with the highest risk items that might happen in your specific environment. There are five high-risk items for firms, specifically. The highest risk area for most firms is business email compromise. The second biggest risk is a ransomware attack. Following ransomware, the next biggest risk is unauthorized access to your network. Last, but certainly not least, we see data breach and wire fraud. You would be surprised at the frequency with which these risks occur.

Let's start with a business email compromise. A malicious actor gets access to your email system, right? They send an email with an attachment attempting to spread the malware to all your customers. What do you do next?

Next, think about ransomware attacks. Imagine you're a victim to a ransomware attack. All of your computers are completely offline and your data is all encrypted and unavailable to you. What do you do next in that scenario?

Third, we have unauthorized access to your network. One of your staff reports that their last login into your customer management system indicates that it came from China. Someone's gained access to your computer system. What do you do in that scenario?

The fourth item is a data breach. Let's say one of your customers contacts you and says that their social security number and contact information was found on the dark web, and they believe that it was leaked from your firm. What do you do in that scenario?

Last is wire fraud. Wire fraud would go something like this. Your CFO received a link from an unknown hacker and just wired $10,000 to their bank account. What's next? What would you do in that scenario?

Taking a look at each one of these five scenarios, think about how to build a plan and what should be included in that plan. Every single incident response plan should include:

1. **Prevention.** Any plan should have some sort of training for your team to make sure that the type of event is less likely to occur to begin with. And this starts with training your employees.

2. **Detection.** This involves reporting suspicious activity and training your employees to make sure they do that.

3. **Containment.** That's preventing the spread of the incident.

4. **Eradication.** This is about getting the hacker out of your network.

Make a plan and start through it. Don't stop there, though. You still need to create a document. This should be a living document that changes over time. This document also needs to be accessible even when your network is offline.

There are a couple of key reasons that you need a document. The first one is simple: consistency. Responding to an event the same way every time allows you to avoid making mistakes when you're upset, worried, tired, and stressed. Believe me, when you have an event like this, you're not in a calm state of mind. It's a hectic situation. Plans are also helpful when they're documented from a reference standpoint, as in during the incident. It's easier to get a step ahead. A reference is going to be critical to keep track of which phase you're in and to make sure that you're moving down the steps in order.

Here's an example. If you started the recovery section of the plan before eradication, then you'd have a real problem. If the hackers are still in the network, and you start recovering everything, you're soon going to be back where you started. The hackers are going to be able to detonate ransomware again somewhere else.

The next piece is expediency. When you have a documented plan, it's a lot easier to get rolling right away. When an incident occurs, the first couple of hours are critical for containment. If you're sitting around trying to remember what to do, you're going to be in real trouble.

Documentation is also helpful when it comes to training. Without a documented plan, training somebody new on the process can be nearly impossible. It is also very helpful for the continuous improvement and education of your current staff. The last step of that incident response plan should be to review the lessons learned. Having a written incident response plan allows you to update the plan regularly.

Documenting a plan is a ton of work. You're probably thinking to yourself, is it worth all the effort? Let's think back to the research for a minute. 71-20=51. How much more work can your firm afford to take on during something like a ransomware attack? I think you'll agree that it is absolutely worth having and documenting a plan.

Now, let's go over disclosing the information. When you experience a cyber-attack, people don't view you as a victim as you would think. I know this isn't fair at all. When the regulators step in, the first thing they think is, how were you negligent? What did you do, or not do, to make this happen to your firm? This is where the FTC regulations kick. It's not enough just to be secure; you also have the regulations you have to worry about. Regulators will come in and scrutinize every single thing. They will view you as guilty until you prove that you have everything documented.

Reacting to being breached by sending out an email that says, "All of our computers are down" doesn't help the perception either. Sending out a message like this destroys credibility and trust. This is where you're going to want to have a documented communication plan as part of your incident response plan. It's going to include things like who's going to communicate, what they're going to say, and when they're going to start communicating.

There are a couple of key points here I want you to think about: transparency, clarity, empathy, timeliness, and guidance. Your communication plan should be very transparent. This is where you start rebuilding trust. You're going to provide accurate and timely information, including things like the nature of the incident, the type of data that was compromised, and the potential impact on those whose information was compromised. Openly acknowledging the breach is key. You're also going to want to make sure that your communication plan keeps in mind clarity. Avoid technical jargon. Try to keep it in plain English and, as much as possible, give clear steps on what can be taken by the victims.

You're also going to want to incorporate empathy. Acknowledge people's concerns; they may be feeling vulnerable, anxious, or even frustrated, and want to make sure that their privacy is a priority for your firm. The communication plan should incorporate timeliness. What I mean by this is you're going to communicate promptly that the event happened, but you're also going to follow a communication cadence and communicate how often they should be expecting updates from you. You're also going to want to include guidance that includes clear steps that minimize further risk for other victims.

Most importantly, make sure that you're not sharing information that you do not know is absolutely truthful and absolutely correct. Go back and confirm everything with the people on the incident response team. If they say that they think something happened, push them until they can say that they know something happened. In your communication, make sure that it is crystal clear.

The next piece is considering who you should have on your team. What this comes down to is who are the people on your team that are going to be involved during a breach? You're also going to want to have a notification plan for the team. How are you going to notify them that the event is taking place? Make sure that you have contact information that is available when your systems are all offline. When you're putting together your firm's incident response plan, here are some people that you should consider.

There will be some people that are part of your incident response team that are outside your organization. You're going to want to make sure that you have some other phone numbers readily available. Who else do you want to alert? Who else might be helping you? This really depends on the nature of the event. I suggest that you create a speed dial list.

The first group that you're going to want to have on that list are law enforcement agencies. Local level law enforcement, including police and cybercrime units, are really important, especially if the event involves a breach of personal identifiable information. As a firm, you're loaded with personal identifiable information. If that sensitive information gets into the wrong hands, that's when the FTC could also become involved.

You're also going to want to have a cybersecurity and infrastructure security agency on your list for the speed dial. They offer resources and assistance for organizations dealing with cyber incidents. They're basically a federal agency that provides guidance and support for critical infrastructure protection, including cyber security.

Furthermore, you're going to want to have incident response service providers on the list. These are the folks capable of doing things like assisting and containing the threat actor. They can also investigate the incident and provide things like forensic investigations to identify the root cause of your breach. Additionally, they can make suggestions to help you prevent future attacks. According to the FBI, 38% get hit a second time after the first incident *(Barracuda International Survey, 2023)*.

Another important number on your list should be your insurance provider. If your firm has cyber insurance, your insurance provider can guide you through the claims process and how to access coverage. However, keep in mind that they will be looking very closely at your network and verifying that the cybersecurity preventative measures you said you had on your application are actually in place during the forensic audit process. This is where a lot of organizations get into trouble and, sadly, don't get coverage.

This is only if you have cyber insurance, which is usually a separate line item and a separate rider for your firm. If you don't have this, you should consider getting it. You're also going to want to help get your insurance policy number and all the details necessary. As a bonus tip, ask your insurance provider if there are specific people that you should have on your incident response list such as legal counsel, incident response service providers, and special law enforcement.

Here's a recap of your speed dial list:

- Law Enforcement Agencies

- Regulatory Authorities

- Incident Response Service Providers

- Your Insurance Provider

Obviously, you're going to also need to notify the victims who were impacted by this breach.

Did you have a plan before you started this session today? If not, there's likely more issues with your cybersecurity program. A lack of incident response plan is a key indicator that your firm has weak cybersecurity. You can measure your cybersecurity program's success and effectiveness by getting a third-party security analysis. Also, I've put together a simple incident response planning checklist that you can get by going to **csoscott. com/incident-response**.

Chapter 8:

Protecting Your Organization's Reputation After An Email Attack

In this chapter, we'll go over protecting your firm's reputation after its email gets hacked.

Having a hacker in your email can do much more damage than you expect. As I stated previously, business email compromise is one of the biggest threats to a small business. This is a very important topic and can be reputation ending. Hopefully, after reading this chapter, you'll be able to take some good things back to your team on improving your cybersecurity posture.

We've all heard the most common scammer story. One of your accounting managers gets a note asking them to buy some gift cards. This type of scam or fraud happens so often, that most people reading this know somebody who's received this type of email or a text message. Why does this tactic keep getting used? Because it works; plain and simple. And it's a much bigger problem than people realize. In this chapter, we're going to talk about more dangerous email tactics that hackers are using.

We've seen an increased number of successful cyber-attacks recently. What makes an attack successful, from a hacker's point of view, is getting the victim to pay. Hackers know that ransomware isn't enough to make that happen every single time, so they do other things like exfiltrate data, which means pull sensitive data out of your servers. It also means doing things like taking down your firm's website. Additionally, it means disrupting your communication methods, keeping you from getting to the outside world to let them know what's going on.

Many of these hackers focus on email to get into their victims' networks. Imagine for a minute if every single person you've ever emailed received a message from you. It would get past their spam filter because it's coming from somebody they trust. It's a simple link. Just viewing the message gives the hacker more information about their next victim. The more savvy people may start contacting you, asking if you sent it to them, while others open the link and end up infecting their own networks. So, what do you do? Do you reach out to everyone to let them know that this is happening? If so, what do you say?

There are more than 300 billion emails sent every single day. The ones that are sent out under your firm's name are the most important ones. Why? The answer is very straightforward. These emails are the lifeblood of the relationship that you have with your clients.

These types of cyber-attacks are happening all the time. The difference between the firm who goes out of business and the one that keeps their client base and continues to grow comes down to one thing: communication. The hackers want into your email because you have sensitive info. Firms often have access to large amounts of sensitive information like customer names, addresses, social security numbers, and financial and credit information. This information is valuable to these criminals. The other thing is that you do financial transactions, which can be lucrative from the standpoint of the cyber criminals.

Also, they want to use you to communicate with your clients. A lot of firms communicate regularly to their clients via email, making it easy for the attacker to use that to phish those clients. Ultimately, your email ends up giving them the opportunity to do things like spread more malware, by sending spam containing malicious files to other people. Once they're in your system, they can access money, by creating fake invoices or payment requests to your clients. They can even trick your contacts into clicking links to spread this malicious software. Furthermore, if they get to the right person inside of your firm, the hackers could impersonate executives and convince people to do things like send money to the wrong people.

The other things that hackers find useful are the pieces of personal information stored in your mailbox. Things like first and last names, addresses, and birthdates are often found within these messages. That's information that the attackers can use to steal identities. They are looking for access to other accounts, and are able to reset passwords through email to access these other accounts.

Ultimately, though, this impacts your clients' trust. This is the most sacred thing that it impacts. We're talking about reputational damage here. It erodes confidence in your firm's ability to protect their information. It means loss of clients, or difficulty attracting new clients. It also impacts your reputation with your employees. Needless to say, you can kiss email marketing goodbye. When you have a breach like this, the attacker uses your email system to send out messages to every single person you've ever communicated with. When you try to do email marketing in the future, you get delayed responses and people second-guess the authenticity of the message that you're sending out. You end up having a bad reputation from a spam standpoint, making it much harder for you to use email marketing to engage any clients.

Let's start with the 7 biggest mistakes that firms make when it comes to these types of breaches:

1. Ignoring the issue.
2. Delaying action.
3. Not reporting the incident.
4. Not informing.
5. Not changing passwords.
6. Falling for the follow-up scams.
7. Overlooking other compromised accounts.

First, we have those who choose to ignore the issue. Many firms ignore the signs of an email compromise because they think it's a minor issue or a one-time occurrence. However, ignoring the problem allows the attacker to continue their activities and cause more damage.

The next mistake is delaying action. Breaches are time-sensitive items. Time is of the essence, and delaying action when dealing with an email compromise can give the attacker much more opportunity to exploit the compromised account.

What about responding to the incident itself? Ultimately, many firms try to handle it themselves, and this can be a mistake. Failing to report, the email compromise to your cybersecurity or support people hinders any potential investigation, and it makes it much more difficult.

Then you have to deal with contacts when an email account gets compromised. The attacker can use an email account to send out malicious messages to all the victim's contacts. Not just their contacts, but every single person that they've ever emailed.

After an email compromise, you need to change your passwords. Some individuals end up having situations where the attacker is able to get into other accounts because they share the same passwords or have similar passwords. There is also the risk of falling for the follow-up emails or scams in which the hacker poses as support representatives to gain more information or to extort money.

What about the other compromised accounts? Sometimes, when hackers gain access to your email, they're able to get access to multiple accounts of that same individual. Focusing only on the compromised email account can really limit the scope of what the actual breach covers.

But what's the biggest mistake when these types of events happen? The biggest mistake is not being prepared. You ultimately end up wasting time trying to figure out what to do. Sometimes, you make hasty emotional decisions and end up making the situation even worse. This is why you want to put together a plan for an email compromise.

When you start to look at the numbers, it becomes obvious. 28% of employees are fooled by malicious emails *(Microsoft, 2023)*. Hackers see this as an opportunity. Also, there has been a 175% increase in two-step phishing attacks on people's email accounts *(Security Today, 2024)*. Furthermore, 71% of organizations experienced an email compromise in 2023 *(ProofPoint, 2024)*. This is even higher for firms because you have a whole host of sensitive information about your clients, which makes you a prime target.

So, how can you prepare your firm for a business email compromise? The answer is pretty straightforward: you start with your users. Hackers know that users are the way into your network. They're going to try to trick a user into opening the door for them, and then bypass the cyber security tools you've worked so hard to put into place.

Let's dig into the red flags all users should know about, and how to spot a phishing email. There's are a number of signs that you can look for:

- Spelling and Grammar Errors
- URLs Not Matching
- Requests for Personal Information
- Generic Greetings
- Sense of Urgency in Demand or Request
- Unexpected Attachments
- Suspicious Sender Address
- Poor Email Formatting
- Offers That Seem Too Good To Be True

What do I mean by poor grammar and spelling? Most phishing emails originate from foreign sources, and as such, they often contain misspelled words or awkward phrasing. These errors make phishing emails a little easier to recognize.

You can check for mismatched URLs by hovering over the link in the email, without clicking it. This causes the destination URL to pop up. If that doesn't match the text of the hyperlink of the company that you're expecting, then that is another red flag.

Also, legitimate organizations don't usually ask for personal information via email. If an email asks for sensitive information, it's probably a scam.

Phishing emails are often seen in large batches, so they often have generic greetings like "Dear Customer". Many companies personalize their emails with your name when they send them out. This can be another way to recognize that the email might be a scam.

Then we have a sense of urgency. Many of these different phishing emails are trying to create a false sense of urgency or panic to prompt the recipient to act quickly, without thinking. That's when mistakes happen. For example, they might say that your account will be closed if you don't respond within an hour.

Also, if you receive an email from an unknown source with an attachment, be suspicious. Never open the attachment. If you open the attachment, you could be opening the door for a hacker to enter your network.

What about the sender's address? Phishing scams often come from an email address that resembles those of legitimate companies, but slightly altered. You might find that the letter "O" in "HOLLY.SMITH@Apple.com" has been changed to the number "0". These subtle changes to the email address are enough to look legitimate, but they are, in fact, a phishing email.

Poorly formatted emails are another red flag. Look for things like the company's logo; is the logo current, or is it an older one? Another sign could be the way in which the email is written. Sometimes the email's formatting might not look like the other emails from that company, which is another sign.

Finally, when an offer is just too good to be true, it probably is. Be especially skeptical of messages claiming that you've won a contest you don't remember entering, that offer exclusive access to incredible deals, or anything of that effect.

Let's walk through what you should do if you get one of these messages. First, don't click on any of the links or download any of the attachments. Do not provide the sender with any personal information. Contact the person or organization who the email allegedly came from and ask if they sent you the email. Finally, report the email to your computer support people and make sure they are aware of it.

What do you do if you've been phished? Most of the time, users don't even know it has happened. If you expect that it has happened, contact your IT or Tech Support immediately. Make sure that you change all of your passwords and monitor your accounts.

There are a number of things that you should be looking for, such as:

- Unusual Logins

- Emails You Didn't Send

- Missing or Deleted Emails

- Unwanted Password Reset Emails

- Changes in Account Settings

- Increased Spam or Phishing Emails

- Unusual Activity in Connected Accounts

- Inability to Access Your Account

Let's go over unusual login activity. Check your email account's login history for any unfamiliar locations or devices that have access to your account. Most email providers offer this feature under account settings. If you see emails in your set folder that you didn't send, or if your contacts report receiving suspicious emails from you, it's a strong indicator of unauthorized access to your email account.

What about missing or deleted messages? Look for important emails disappearing from your inbox or folders without your intervention. This could be a sign that you have a compromised email account.

The other sign to look for is receiving a password reset or account recovery email that you didn't initiate. That indicates someone is attempting to take control of one or more of your accounts.

What about emails from unknown senders with attachments or links? Be especially cautious if you receive emails from an unknown sender. If it has an attachment or link in it, the email could be a phishing attempt or contain malware.

Also, look for changes in account settings. If you notice unexpected changes in your account settings, such as an alternative email address, phone number, or forwarding rules, your account is likely compromised.

Next, you're going to see an increase in spam or phishing emails. A hacked email account may often be used to send spam emails to your clients, but also it's likely to end up getting a lot more spam and phishing emails while the attacker tries to cover its tracks.

What about unusual activity for connected accounts? As you know, your email account is linked to other online services like social media, online shopping, etc. This is why you should check for any suspicious activity in those accounts as well.

Finally, if you suddenly find yourself unable to log into your email account, it's a pretty good sign that an attacker could have changed your password. This is something that you're definitely going to want to look into further. Make sure you bring your computer support people into the conversation if this happens.

What do you do, though, if you see one of these different things happening, and your account has been compromised? Follow an incident response plan. An incident response plan should include things like:

- Prevention
- Training Employees on How to Avoid These Traps

- Detection

- Reporting Suspicious Activity

- Containment. This involves preventing the spread of the incident.

- Eradication. This means getting the attacker out of your email.

- Recovery. For this, you'll be getting your email back up and going so that you have all the messages you expected.

- Notifying anybody that probably has or will receive one of those messages.

- Lessons learned. This is about improving the plan.

Containment, eradication, and recovery will be taken care of by your support team. That leaves you with one major step, which is notification. You're going to be responsible for letting all those people who are in your email know that you're dealing with this type of targeted attack. Are you going to say to them, "Oh my gosh, we've been hacked!"? Of course not. Instead, you're going to have a simple notification email.

The email will have a subject that says something to the effect of "cyber security incident." Then it's going to have an announcement explaining the breach. You're going to want to lead with something along the lines of, "We're writing to inform you that despite our security measures, our firm has experienced a targeted cyber-attack. While we are still in the early stages of investigation, we want to assure you that the security and privacy of your information remains our highest priority. So far, our investigation has revealed that attackers may have been able to access your email address. Please exercise vigilance when opening attachments or links that you don't expect, especially from somebody you don't recognize. As an extra level of precaution, please note the following: Don't update your payment information for wires or ACH without contacting the requesting party on a known or published phone number. Do not use phone numbers provided via email like those in the attachment or the sender's signature.

We appreciate your understanding, patience, and continued support as we resolve and restore normal operations. Please contact me directly with any questions or concerns."

That's a pretty easy email, but what do we see going wrong here? Well, a couple of things. For one thing, there's a delay in disclosure, as in failing to promptly notify or inform all the people about the cyber-attack. This ends up eroding your trust with them, and leaving them vulnerable as well to further attacks. We also see a lack of transparency. Being vague or evasive in the communication can spread suspicion and mistrust. Being transparent about the nature and the extent of the cyber-attack and the data that might have been compromised can help build that trust. Ultimately, when you talk about the actions that are being taken to resolve the situation, they start to feel a little bit more secure. They start to feel that you're doing the right things to help alleviate this event.

Another mistake that we see is when people minimize the impact. They downplay the severity of the cyber-attack or its consequences. This can harm your credibility and communication, and ultimately harm your firm.

While communicating, people often mess up by using technical jargon. They use complex technical language that confuses the audience, and makes it difficult for non-technical stakeholders to understand the situation fully. Sometimes people skip over giving guidance. After a cyber-attack, affected individuals need guidance on how to protect themselves. They also need support in dealing with the consequences of the attack.

You should also avoid providing contradictory statements. Providing inconsistent information through various channels creates confusion and undermines the credibility of the communication that you're sending out.

The final mistake that we'll go over is skipping the internal communication, which means communicating to your own team what to say to people who are contacting your firm with questions. Also, some people miss giving the employees in your firm a heads up that this is even happening. This allows the attacker to utilize your relationships with those people to further their attack.

What are the next steps for you? First, make sure to follow your incident response plan. This plan was created precisely for moments like these. Next, ensure everyone involved is updated throughout the event. Communication is key, and keeping everyone in the know is critical. Lastly, take time to learn from this event, and contemplate how you can prevent another attack like this from happening again in the future. Review each of the steps in your incident response plan and figure out how to make things better for the next time around.

Do you have an incident response plan? Have you put together a response for what happens when somebody gets into one of your email accounts and sends out a bunch of messages? I have an easy way that you can get started on this today. We put together a free business email compromise planning kit for you. It includes a number of emails that you can use for notification, as well as scripts that you can use if people contact you with this type of event. If you're interested in this, go to **csoscott.com/email-compromise** and get your free downloads. It includes a training guide, communication steps, as well as email templates to save you time building your own email response plan.

Chapter 9:

An Executive's Guide To Protecting Critical Data Assets In a Firm

In this chapter, I'm going to cover protecting your critical data assets, which is a very important topic for every business, but particularly CPA and Law Firms.

You're probably wondering what a critical asset is. You're probably even thinking to yourself that sounds like something IT people would be responsible for. The critical data asset is a specific type of data that is most crucial to running your business. So no, this is not just an IT issue. Everyone in your operation would be impacted if this data either disappeared, was modified, or just became unavailable in some way. Everyone in your firm owns this, and your firm has a ton of critical data.

Let's start with data assets. This is the data that you take for granted. It might be desktop files, downloaded items, or things that are in your documents. Those are important, but they're not quite as important as what we're going to get to later in this chapter. Without these, you'd have a difficult time getting your day going. You might lose work, and you might have to redo something. You might have to rewrite a document. You might have to rewrite a contract. Even though you would be personally impacted, losing these data assets wouldn't impact your entire firm. In fact, your firm probably wouldn't even miss a beat. These are data assets, and they're important.

But there's another type of asset. These assets are much more important. Those are your critical data assets. I want you to think of these as the crown jewels of your firm. They're critical to your relationship with your employees, your vendors, and your clients. Protecting critical data assets is imperative to your firm's survival.

Let me give you an example. Recently, a firm contacted us because they had a problem. They were running into a situation where a number of their clients were receiving emails stating that they needed to change their payment info. They appeared to be coming from the firm itself. Somebody had gotten a hold of their marketing list and were sending out these emails to people that they knew that the firm was working with. The hackers were able to make a slight modification to the email domain, so it looked like it was coming from the firm. Imagine changing one little letter in your return address. This might not be something that most people would recognize.

The firm had a really big problem on their hands, as the customers started interacting with these folks and making changes to their billing information. As a result, some of them were missing payments to the firm. Can you imagine what kind of mess this created? And it was all because of a simple bit of critical data that the attackers were able to get to. This stuff doesn't even sound that important. This was just stuff in their CRM. How important can this be to the relationships with your clients? The answer is: very important.

What can you do personally to protect these data assets? The easiest way hackers get this info is tricking you into clicking a link. The more authority you have in your firm, the more of a target you are. How do hackers get you to click these links? They look for publicly available info about you. They might even impersonate one of your friends on Facebook, just to learn as much as they can. They use this knowledge to create targeted messages for you. These messages could come in your email, in social media, or even as a text message.

How do you protect yourself? Never click on a message you do not expect, even if it's from someone you trust. Your personal info is almost as important as your firm's, because hackers use it to get to your firm.

We're going to talk about three different things in this chapter that your organization can do. We're going to talk about identification, protection, and management of those critical data assets. To start, how do you identify your firm's critical data assets? One way to do that is to think about the data that your firm just couldn't live without. I have some good news for you. Most firms have similar critical data assets:

- Client's Personal Data
- PII (Personal Identifying Information) of Clients & Employees
  - Names
  - Addresses
  - Contact Information
  - Social Security Numbers
  - Tax Identification Numbers
- Firm's Financial Records (bank statements, investment portfolios, and loan documents)
- Wills and Trust Information
- Business Client Data
- Company Financial Statements
- Balance Sheets
- Income Statements
- Cash FlowStatements
- Notes to Accounts (usernames, passwords, codes, etc)
- Firm's Tax Returns (past and current filings)
- Support Schedules and Related Documentations
- Audit Documentation
- Audit Plans
- Working papers
- Audit Reports
- Audit Findings
- Firm's Payroll Records
- Firm's Employee Compensation

- Firm's Deductions & Benefits Data
- Communication Records
- Client Correspondence
- Records of:
  - Emails
  - Letters
  - Memos
  - Meeting Notes
  - Recommendations
- Regulatory Communication
- Correspondence from:
  - Tax Authorities
  - Financial Institutions
  - Regulatory Bodies
- Employee Specifics:
  - Hiring Dates
  - Job Roles
  - Salaries
  - Employee Performance Reviews
  - Training Records
  - Professional Credentials
  - Certifications
  - Continuing Professional Education Records
- Billing & Financial Data
- Client Billing Records

- Service Fees

- Payment Terms

- Invoices

- Payments Received

- Financial Records

- Firm's Revenue & Expenses

- Profit & Loss Statements

- Firm's Budgets

- Tax Codes

- Firm's Laws & Regulations

- Accounting Standards, Guidelines, and Best practices

- Subscription-Based Research Tools and Databases

- Client Portals & Digital Access Logs

- Access and activity logs for client portals and platforms where the clients can upload or download their financial documents

- Security Protocols & Encryption Keys for Client Portals

- Client leads that have information on potential clients who inquired or showed interest

- Campaign Analytics (This is where you have performance metrics for advertising and promo efforts)

- Licensing & Accreditation Details (for your firm and individual accountants)

- Audit Trail Record

- Detailed, time-stamped records of all actions taken on critical data (often required for regulatory compliance)

- Records of Any Ethics or Regulatory Inquiries or Concerns

- Technology and Security Data

- Software Licenses
- Configuration for:
  - Accounting Software
  - Tax preparation tools
  - Audit software
- Backup and recovery protocols, as well as the strategies and records related to the data backups, recovery tests, and disaster recovery plans

These are pretty much the standard critical data assets, but there could be more at your firm. What you're going to want to do is start by identifying that data. The next step is to figure out the value of that data. Remember, the value of the critical data assets is much more than just the cost to replace it. Think about those critical data assets I listed above.

Let's use employee data as an example. What's the real impact of an employee data breach? There would be a direct financial loss, like the money spent in the remediation, recovery, and/or notification. Maybe there are legal fines, or identify theft protection costs.

But what about indirect financial loss? This includes things like lost productivity, decrease in employee morale, or additional training and time spent in training. What about operational loss, disruption of daily operations, crisis management, employee concerns, and distractions? Just imagine everybody sitting around talking about this breach you've experienced. Ultimately, this also means an increased workload for a number of folks on your team who are dealing with this incident directly. Think about what your human resources team would have to go through.

What about reputational loss via media impact? Imagine a news truck showing up in your parking lot, and you have to talk to the media about what's happening. You might have concerns from your customers, as they begin to learn about the event. At this point, you have long-term brand damage. If this is sitting on the internet, it's going to pop up over and over again when people search for your firm. All that from a simple employee data breach. And this is just for your employee data. We didn't even get into any of the compliance or regulatory impact. These are the type of events that lead to compliance police showing up at your door with a magnifying glass. Is there a long-term strategic plan for this type of loss?

You're going to have to have some major conversations with your stakeholders. You're going to have to go to reassure them that everything's okay. You may have increased reporting from a regulatory standpoint. Ultimately, you'll need to undergo a strategic reprioritization in order to better protect this data moving forward.

Now let's talk about the impact if other critical data assets were to be compromised. What should determine that impact? How do you determine what the impact would be? These answers are determined by the person who owns or manages a particular critical data asset. For example, who's responsible for the employee data that we just discussed in your firm? This person should also be responsible for understanding how the ownership of these critical data assets impacts the organization, particularly if compromised. So why do we want it to have an owner? It gives you somebody to go and speak to, if needed. It also makes the owner have some accountability for the data asset, as well as the protections that are in place around it. Last, but certainly not least, it provides that person with some additional authority, as they're going to determine the impact of the breach of their critical data asset on your firm.

Let's go take a look at the protection aspect of this equation. How are you protecting the data? What do I mean by protecting, you may ask? There are three different aspects when it comes to protecting this sort of data: confidentiality, integrity, and availability. If a hacker broke into your firm, is there data that you just don't want them to see? If so, protecting that data is creating confidentiality. It's a critical aspect in making sure things like sensitive info about your employees are being protected. This should also include sensitive info about customers and the type of jobs and information that your firm works on.

Next we have integrity. What data in your firm would you not want anyone able to change or forge? Protecting this data would be protecting its integrity. Think about things like the agreements, contracts, and commitments that you've made. Ultimately, you want to make sure that those do not get changed over time.

Finally, we have availability. What are the things that you need to make sure are available to you every single day in order to run your firm? These are the things that would cause your business to come to a complete stop if they were offline or unavailable. Think about things like access to your customer management portal or your service portal. Protecting your data is about ensuring availability.

Confidentiality, integrity, and availability are the building blocks for protecting any of the critical data assets in your environment. But how do they work? How do you actually protect these assets? This is where your cybersecurity program really comes into play. Let's go over a couple of examples.

In terms of confidentiality, one of the most common examples is multi-factor authentication. There's encryption and data loss prevention systems. This makes sure that those critical data assets stay confidential. Then we have integrity like secure network protocols, backups, and recovery solutions. An example of integrity would be user training. These are different tools that are in place to make sure your employees know how to keep these critical data assets secure. Then, finally, we have availability. These are things like failover internet, power redundancy, and cloud storage. Again, make sure that you have access to the critical data that your firm needs to run daily.

A lot of times, the question I ask firms when I'm in the discovery process is, what impact would a connectivity outage have on your day-to-day operation? In other words, if the internet went down right now, what applications or people would be impacted? Who would run into your office screaming the loudest? That's how you determine the priorities.

Your investment should be based on the actual value of the critical data assets inside of your specific firm. Value really means impact. Ultimately, this comes down to risk. Risk is measured based on the impact and likelihood, or the value of the critical assets, and how likely it is to be taken away, damaged, or even somehow extracted from your environment.

So on the impact side, we have things like high impact. High impact risks could cause a major problem in your organization. Next, we have medium impact risks. Medium impact risks usually result in a serious or adverse effect. Finally, we have low impact risks, which involve a limited impact on your environment. Then we have the likelihood of the breach occurring. High likelihood would be something like one to ten times a year, and low likelihood will be maybe once every couple of years.

You can take your critical data assets and chart them out based on the impact and likelihood of something bad happening to them. Ultimately, higher risk calls for higher security investment. So when you're thinking about protecting critical data assets, it's a major component of your plan. The priority is to figure out the likelihood.

Now, let's explore managing those critical data assets. Data assets have a life cycle. Management of critical data assets comes down to defining steps in the life cycle. It also starts with creation or collection, then classification access, as in controlling who has access to it. Take into consideration storage, usage, transmission, archiving, and disposal.

In terms of creation, we want to know which data have been created or collected inside of your firm. Then we have classification. What types of methods are used to identify this critical information? This is especially important for sensitive information that you're trying to protect from a confidentiality standpoint. Next, we have access. Who in your organization has permission to view or edit this data? After we've considered access, we need to consider storage. How is the critical data stored? In addition, we have usage and transmission. What can users do and not do with this data? How is this data shared between your system, vendors, or other people inside of your organization? Next, you'll want to consider archiving. How is this data kept after it's done being used? Finally, we have disposal. How long do you keep it for before it slips into the final stage, disposal? When is the data destroyed, and how is it disposed of? This may not sound super important to you, but here's a situation that happened about a year ago. We were contacted by a firm who had a little problem. They were working with an outsourced IT MSP company who were replacing all of the laptops that their sales team used. In the process, they also replaced a number of laptops the executive teams used as well. Well, come to find out, one of the folks in that MSP ended up going through and selling those laptops on eBay. In the process, they didn't do a great job of destroying the data on the drives. Someone bought one of those laptops, specifically the one that the CFO used, and then proceeded to reach out to clients about payments. This is why it's so critical to have a plan when it comes to every phase of this, including the destruction phase of old equipment.

The first step to get started with all of this is identifying each of your critical data assets, as well as the owners of each of those assets. Then you're going to want to analyze the impact of each of those critical assets to see what would happen if it's lost, modified, or leaked. Next, you create a security plan based on that impact. Ultimately, it comes down to managing the asset's life cycle.

It seems complicated, but there's an easy way to get started on this. We've created a free critical data asset evaluation form. All you need to do is go to **csoscott.com/data-assets**. This is going to help you to identify those critical data assets, how to protect them, and how to manage them.

Chapter 10:

Stop, Drop, and Roll: Easy Steps Every Firm's CFO Should Know for Incident Readiness

In this chapter, I will cover incident response readiness, a very important topic that hopefully you'll never have to use. Stop, drop, and roll.

These are the easy steps that every firm CFO should know for an incident response readiness. Basically, we're talking about building out and using tabletop exercises to put together a plan and a recovery, so when, heaven forbid, an incident happens, you know just what to do.

Throughout my years in the industry, there are two huge mistakes I see organizations make. The biggest mistake I see firms making is thinking that because they already have somebody they pay to take care of all of their IT needs, they themselves don't need to focus on it. Far too often, a general MSP or IT person, to no fault of theirs, is not able to cover all the bases. That's why the FTC stepped in. Recently, the FTC imposed some major regulations that have some serious consequences; consequences that directly affect you. So many firms were thinking they were properly protected, and they weren't. They had sensitive consumer data that was getting leaked. As I said in previous chapters, data breaches resulting in the leaking of sensitive information occur, on average, every 11 seconds *(CyberSecurity Ventures, 2023)*. That's the same frequency as car accidents! For those of you who have your firms in California, the rate of breaches in California is double the national average; it's one every five and a half seconds *(IC3 Report, 2022)*.

Let me ask you this simple question: would you drive your car daily and not have any car insurance on it? Probably not, because of the impact it would have on your finances if there were an accident. If we got into an accident and we had to pay out of pocket, it might impact our home. Now, how much more important for your firm, where people depend on you for their livelihood and your clients and your reputation that you took so many years to build? Mistake number one for incident response readiness is thinking that you have it covered. That's why now it's mandatory to have vulnerability risk assessments done once a year.

The second mistake is the key mistake we see executives make. This mistake is saying that you're too busy. Imagine if you came in to work and everything was locked down. You know, you suddenly have a lot of time on your hands when that happens and when we're brought in post-breach to remediate and help the firm get back up. It's just crippling. I understand running a firm as an executive. Like I said earlier in this book, we're all dodging bullets all the time, between the recession, inflation, employment rules and regulations, and your busy client deadlines. Let me tell you, though; nothing is a bigger risk to your business than a cyber incident. It's just so sudden. With that, let's jump in and talk about incident response.

Most of what we talk about and focus on involves prevention. However, how you recover is equally, if not more, important. This is something you want to be proactive about, so that you are prepared ahead of time. Ask yourself, if your firm got hit by hackers tomorrow, could you actually recover? Could you immediately get back online? Without a plan, recovery is very unlikely. Did you know that more than 45% of firms don't have a plan *(FRSecure, 2022)*? The thing is, the price of not having a plan is pretty impactful on a firm. Obviously, it impacts the amount of time it takes to get you back online, which can directly affect the operation of your business. It's also going to impact the amount of money that you spend to get back online. So not having a plan is going to cost you substantially more, as it takes you longer to decide what to do after the breach has already happened. Ultimately, it could also cost you your reputation, because if you don't have a plan in place, it's going to become apparent the longer it takes to get your business operational again.

You're probably thinking to yourself, but isn't this an IT thing? Your IT provider might have a written plan they follow to get your computers back online, but even if they do, there's a lot more at stake here. It is not just about getting your computers back online. This impacts your entire firm. It's about fully recovering, so it's much bigger than just your IT department. It's not IT who's going to be facing the public and communicating with your clients. Oftentimes, if an incident occurs, it's your firm that is going to be in the media spotlight. Somebody on the executive team is going to have to be the face of the entire disaster: that's going to be you. Who's going to be getting the calls when the incident happens? Chances are, again, that's going to be somebody on the executive's team. Who is going to make the major operational decisions on how the firm is going to respond to the incident? Again, somebody on the executive team. Do you really want to be making decisions in the heat of the moment that could decide the fate of your firm?

You wouldn't want to plan for a fire during the fire, right? Remember back when you were a kid? Your school didn't wait for you to catch on fire before they taught you about stop, drop and roll, right? Knowing what to do and how to react when faced with an emergency is key to survival. It can be crucial for your cyber survival, as well. When an incident occurs, you can do the same steps. Stop what you're doing, drop all your current work, and roll out that incident response plan. It's a very, very simple protocol that you, as a CFO, should be communicating to the rest of the people in your firm.

But wait! You're thinking to yourself, I don't have an incident response plan and I don't know where to even begin. In this chapter, we're going to dig into how to create an incident response plan for your firm. It starts with something called a tabletop exercise.

A tabletop exercise is an opportunity for your firm to simulate the incident. It gives your entire team the chance to work through an incident. Let me just give you a couple of examples of some valuable tabletop exercises to consider. You might do one for something like a phishing attack, where you send phishing emails to employees and see if they click on any links or attachments. Another example might be a supply chain attack, where somebody uses the tools in your computer system to access all your data. You might do one for a ransomware attack, where everything is locked down. In this scenario, every single device in your network is completely locked down and you can't get access to any of your data. You could also do a scenario where you simulate a disgruntled employee sabotaging your system.

You're probably thinking to yourself that none of these things would ever happen. Isn't this just a waste of time? Executives and business leaders like yourself are super busy. However, when you put together a plan, and you practice a plan, you end up learning much more than if you just put it together. If your firm doesn't prepare, it may not survive. It's that simple.

We recently performed a simple tabletop exercise for a small firm. They thought that they were too small, but during the tabletop exercise, they took three key things away that allowed them to create a great plan. The first one was how to effectively identify an incident. The second was the significance of clearly assigning roles to people inside of their organization. Third, they came up with a specific response plan for different types of incidents. These are just three things that this small firm learned from the practice and doing these tabletop exercises. You'll have similar results. Your firm will benefit.

How do I know? Because we performed a tabletop exercise for a very large, 14-location firm. The CFO had told us that they just didn't have time to do any of this. We were able to get them to do it because their cyber insurance policy actually required that they have this in place. Halfway through the exercise, the CFO was scrambling to figure out what to say. We were simulating the process for if ransomware hit the organization. We were going through and figuring out what all the steps were, and there were several details that they didn't even expect to arise.

The first one was that the whole thing went down on a Wednesday, and payroll was due on a Thursday. The IT team didn't know when the servers were going to be able to come back online, and they needed to develop a tactical way to send out payroll. Not just that, they needed to come up with a way to communicate with the entire staff, since their email and phones were offline. I remember the CFO looking at me and saying, "I didn't know this was going to be such a problem."

Ultimately, they put together their plan, and they re-did the exercise six months later. They were able to work through each of those different pieces. This is why it's so important to perform a tabletop exercise, and not just put together an incident response plan without doing one. You learn so much as you actually go through the exercise.

What other benefits does a tabletop exercise provide? One of the biggest benefits of a tabletop exercise is that it allows you to uncover issues you didn't foresee. Another benefit is that it establishes objectives for incident responses. Furthermore, it strengthens the decision-making skills of the individuals that are going to have to deal with the actual incident, and provides clarity for all of your team members.

Who should participate if you decided to do a tabletop exercise? You're going to want to start with your incident response team. These are the people that are responsible for the event, when it actually occurs. You're also going to want to make sure to include vendors that you rely on for things like IT or cybersecurity. Being prepared for an incident requires a huge team effort.

You should do these tabletop exercises at least once a year. What we found works the best is tying it back to a specific time each year. My favorite thing to do is to tie it to Halloween. It's super simple. You just remember it's Halloween. It's time to go through and review our incident response plan. It's also time to go through and do a tabletop exercise to test that out, because nothing is scarier than having an incident and not having an incident response plan that you've gone through with a tabletop exercise.

What happens when a firm doesn't go through and put together a tabletop? Once, we were called into a firm in February, of all times. They had their system breached. What happened is that hackers were filing false claims on their behalf. The IRS caught wind of this, and they actually blocked the firm's ability to file electronically until this was resolved. The CFO in this situation didn't have an incident response plan, and no one knew what to do or who to call in this scenario. We were brought in afterwards.

A lot of mixed messages were being released. The staff didn't know what to relay to the clients; they didn't even know what their own role was during the breach. The IT team cannot anticipate how your team is going to react. This is why it's critical to not think of this as an IT issue, since it impacts the entire team.

So, how do you conduct a tabletop exercise? As a CFO, this is a major thing that you're going to want to consider as you put together your plan for the next 12 months. I'm going to go through three different areas in this chapter: before, during, and after a simulated event.

Before the simulation starts, you're going to want to create an attendee list and confirm that people are going to be able to make it. You're also going to want to organize the physical setup of the room and schedule the time that you're going to do the event. You're going to want to review the exercise documents and ensure they're clear, complete, and available. Don't forget to explain why you're doing it. I would also suggest that you share the scenario ahead of time so that they can start preparing themselves mentally. This is especially important if this is the first one that your firm has ever gone through.

Next, let's go over what you do during the simulation. You're going to begin with introductions for the participants and the goal of the exercise. I also like to start off these exercises with an explanation of the actual event that's being simulated. Encourage people to get in the mindset of problem-solving. Have the team figure out how to recognize what's happening, and possibly which one of your incident response plans they should start using. The other thing that can be helpful is putting together 5 to 10 injections, or simple items that you plan to add to the exercise, if the team is able to sort out all the other issues that are happening. Controlling the pace and flow of the actual exercise, you'll also want to plan to stimulate discussions to draw answers and solutions from the group, rather than just supplying them.

After this exercise is when the real results come together. First, you're going to want to review the results. Then, you'll need to put together a to-do list that can be distributed to all of the attendees. Be sure to update all your documentation, because I guarantee you, there will be areas you can improve. Then, you're going to want to schedule your next tabletop exercise.

Remember that there are roles and responsibilities inside the tabletop exercise. The first thing that we have are the players. These are the folks that are going to be actively discussing or performing their regular roles and responsibilities during this exercise. They're going to be the ones that are going to initiate the actual plan when a real incident occurs. The other players we have are the observers. These are the folks that are not going to necessarily participate in the exercise, however, they may ask questions or provide subject matter expertise to support the development of player responsibilities to the simulation. Finally, you're going to have facilitators. Your facilitators are going to go through and provide updates to the simulation and moderate discussions. These folks also provide additional information or resolve questions as required. Key exercise planning team members also may assist with facilitation as subject matter experts during the exercise itself.

There's one other group that you may want to consider having as part of your tabletop exercise, depending on the size of your firm, and that's the evaluators. These folks are going to be the ones that are assigned to observe and document certain objectives during the exercise. Their primary responsibility is to document player discussions, as well as procedures that you put together within your incident response plan. One thing worth noting here is that instead of having an evaluation during tabletop exercises, we found a lot of our firms that we work with really enjoy using something like Teams, GoToMeeting, or some other sort of virtual discussion, and recording the entire thing during the tabletop exercise. This makes it so you can go back and evaluate pieces after the fact.

There are a couple other tips that I'll mention here. First, you're going to want to spend time making sure that you're really clear on the objectives and the outcomes. Think through scenarios that are meaningful to your firm specifically, and use those during your tabletop exercises. Also, you're going to want to encourage honesty amongst the team. Meaning if we don't have a solution for something, let's admit it. If you have to go through and ad lib a solution, let's document what the solution is. One thing that we found works very well is to have an outside facilitator that's not part of your organization facilitate these scenarios and tabletop exercises with the team.

The ground rules are pretty straightforward. You're going to stay mentally and physically present throughout this exercise. You're going to silence your phones and close your laptops. You can use a couple of breaks to check messages, but we really recommend you keep these at a minimum. You're also going to want to make sure that everybody is contributing to the discussion. Give everyone the opportunity to participate. One of the things that I like to start our exercises off with is reminding people to have an open mindset and set biases aside. Take a couple of seconds to document what you're going to say before saying it. Also, make sure that you stay on point and on time as you're running the exercise. Remember, ultimately this comes down to continuous improvement, meaning that doing the tabletop exercises and writing a plan is not the end. You're going to go through and improve your next version of your incident response plan.

After the tabletop exercise, you're going to do five simple steps.

1. Make your plan.
2. Document your plan.
3. Disclose strategically.
4. Know your team and who's going to be included.
5. Know who to call.

This means going through and using the tabletop exercise to create your incident response plan. Then you're going to document that plan. This means creating an accessible document, something that you can get to even if all of your servers and all of your different devices are offline. Then, you're going to disclose strategically. Also, you're going to go through and create a communication plan about what you're going to do if or when the event happens. Ultimately, what it comes down to is disclosing information in a strategic manner, because you don't want to give out information that might hinder the investigation that's happening during a cybersecurity event.

The next piece is identifying the people who are going to be involved if the incident happens. I suggest having some slight variations in those teams, depending on the type of incident you're dealing with. Also, you'll want to have a notification plan to get that team engaged. Ultimately, you're going to want to make sure you have contact information available, even if all your systems are offline.

Finally, when it comes to tabletop exercise, it's important that you put together a plan and clarify who needs to get notified and called when the incident starts. Also, you need to know how you're going to identify that an incident is actually happening. This increases your firm's success.

Remember, organizations that have a ransomware recovery plan in place can recover from an attack in an average of 20 days, compared to organizations that don't have a plan, which take an average 71 days. Think about how much work your firm gets done in 71 days. This is all about giving your team the opportunity for success. Being prepared for a cyber attack can help you make the right decisions at the right and crucial time.

We have a simple tabletop exercise that you can download for free at **csoscott.com/tabletop**. It's a great resource to just help you get the ball rolling on your own with your team. Incident response planning can be overwhelming, and ignoring it sets your firm up for a disaster. The good news is that you don't have to go at it alone.

Chapter 11:

Cyber Insurance
And Your Firm

In this chapter, I'm going to talk about cyber insurance for your firm. This is what every managing partner needs to know to survive a claim.

There's so much misinformation and misconceptions of insurance, one of the most important safety nets in case your business gets hit with an incident. I'm proud of you for reading this chapter right now, because obviously you understand how important this is.

In previous chapters, I've mentioned ducking bullets to run your firm. But with a cyber incident, unfortunately, it's immediate and it's instant. Your last safety net is your cyber insurance. If it's not done right, your policy won't be valid when you need it the most.

So, could your firm survive a claim? Think about how well you understand cyber insurance. Insurance is a critical component of any risk mitigation strategy. We're all familiar with getting it. We all have it for things like a car, our house, and other aspects of our business. Why the heck wouldn't we have it for cyber protection? You buy it to transfer risk, which is the same reason you get it for your house and other things. A lot of people think that cyber insurance is already built into their business insurance, but it's not. It's actually a separate policy, which you have to purchase if you want to be able to transfer risk when it comes time for cyber events. When I talk about a cyber event, I'm talking about things like ransomware or having somebody trick one of your users into wiring them $20,000. These are all events that are covered by a specific policy that's just for cyber insurance.

Unlike other types of insurance, when it comes to cyber, it could blow up in your face if not done correctly. What do I mean by that? You're probably familiar with the concept of pre-existing conditions with your health insurance. Imagine you're trying to get health insurance coverage payout. Maybe you have to go to the hospital for something. Your insurance company should cover everything, right? It's straightforward until they realize that you had a pre-existing condition you didn't report.

Hence the complication that's added when it comes to cyber insurance when you need it the most. If a pre-existing condition is in your network, would you even know about it? Would the cyber insurance company even listen to you if you said that you didn't know it was there? Ultimately, they're going to ask you a number of questions. If you didn't know the answer, or you answered incorrectly, do you think they're going to cover you? Nope.

Before we get started on the process of getting cyber insurance, you have a very important question to answer next. Does your firm have any pre-existing conditions? What are you going to use to answer that question? Just to give you an idea of what we're seeing right now nationwide, of the networks that we analyzed in a recent 60-day period, 52% had a pre-existing condition. That would block their ability to submit a claim. Of those 52%, none of them realized it prior. So, if you want to be able to survive a claim, this is something that you're going to want to act on now. You want the benefits, like the ability to transfer risk and to create a viable recovery. You also want business relationships. 60% of businesses say that they would reconsider entering a partnership or an agreement with another business or supplier if the organization did not have comprehensive cyber insurance.

Getting this coverage isn't nearly as easy as getting car insurance, like you may be used to. What is an effective method for approaching cyber insurance? Build a compliance plan. Treat it just like any other compliance that your organization is having to deal with.

Let's think about what we know about health insurance, since that's the easiest to compare. What would you do in order to get in shape before getting health insurance? Would you do an exercise plan, or would you possibly go on a diet? Being healthy is about creating the right rules and following them. Compliance is similar, in this regard, and you have to take the appropriate steps to address the areas of concern.

It can help to understand the reasons for these concerns. Health insurers want an accurate picture so they can balance their payouts. Right now, the cyber insurance industry is in a period of dramatic change. It's a relatively young field, and situations surrounding complaints are constantly changing as hackers continue to change and come up with different ways into networks. Originally, cyber insurance relied on self-reporting, and what they've realized is that it isn't working. So, they've shifted to a more objective approach and tightened their standards.

There are basically six things that every cyber insurance policy is going to ask you before you're able to get coverage:

1. Do you have strong access controls?

2. Do you have regular vulnerability risk assessments happening?

3. Do you have an incident response plan in place?

4. Do you have employee cybersecurity training?

5. Do you have multi-factor authentication in place?

6. Do you use encryption?

Let's take a closer look at each one of these six items. First, let's begin with access controls. These are guards against unauthorized access to sensitive data and systems. They can do a number of things like determine which information a particular user has access to, and verify users' identities.

Insurance companies are also looking for you to have regular vulnerability assessments. That means your firm is going to have an analysis of the environment on a quarterly, if not monthly, basis.

You're going to need an incident response plan, documenting the protocols that your firm is going to go through if an event happens. This plan is all about taking the right actions to contain the situation that is already occurring and, bottom line, limit the damage.

Employee Training is also incredibly important. Security is a team effort. One of the fundamental components to your firm's defense against hackers is cyber awareness training for all of your team members. The multi-million dollar attack on MGM resorts in September 2023 is a great example of the significance of constant training.

Then there's multi-factor authentication. This provides a layer of protection by requiring users to provide two forms of verification before getting access to your systems or data. The first one is typically a password or a PIN. The second one is more difficult, often impossible for hackers to get their hands on, like a physical token on a device, a fingerprint, or maybe some biometric marker.

The other thing that we want to make sure we are doing is encrypting information. Encryption is basically the secret code that protects your organization's information. It defends data at rest, as well as data that's in transport. Meaning if a file is on your file system or if the file's moving across the network, it's still protected.

You might be asking yourself, what type of insurance should I get, and for how much? There are two different types, first party and third party. First party is the type of insurance that covers the cost associated with investing and responding to a cyber event against your organization, as well as the financial impact on an organization's business operations. On the flip side, we have third-party. If your organization experiences damages as a result of another person or organization experiencing a cyber attack, third party insurance provides your organization coverage.

How much coverage does your organization actually need? There are a lot of factors to consider when planning for a cyber event. For one, there's recovery costs, like how much is it going to cost to recover from the event? There's also the amount of sensitive data that your firm has, and your firm's annual revenue. Ultimately, it's not a one-size-fits-all situation.

Your firm is a target for hackers because of the type of information or customer data that you're handling. We're seeing that across the board, due to the ease of phishing one's way into a firm's account. Consider all the confidential information that's stored in your firm in order to service your clients. For the insurer, the cybersecurity protections that you have in place impact how the insurer calculates an organization's policy pricings. You need to consider how much you should get from this coverage. Finally, what types of potential lawsuits, fines, and data recovery costs will be involved in the recovery?

Like I said, this is not a one-size-fits-all situation. There are basically two mistakes that we see all the time. The first one is pretty simple: assuming that basic security is sufficient to qualify for coverage. It isn't. Everybody out there has a firewall and antivirus. Insurance carriers are demanding a lot more. The other mistake that we see people making is believing that you're a safe bet for carriers simply because you're a relatively small business. Actually, carriers see smaller businesses as bigger risks, precisely because they typically under-invest in things like cyber defense.

So, how do you negotiate the best price to get the right coverage? There are basically six things that you're going to want to go through when you're negotiating the right insurance policy for your firm.

1. Only buy what you need.

2. Review all the limits of liability that the insurer is putting into the agreement.

3. Make sure that you obtain retroactive coverage.

4. Make sure that you're paying attention to things like panel and consent provisions.

5. Know how defense costs are allocated.

And finally, you're going to want to obtain coverage from a vendor for acts and omissions. If one of your vendors drops the ball and the attacker gets in, you want to make sure that you're covered.

How do you get prepared? First, you're going to want to make sure that you're ready to answer all of the insurer's underwriting questions. It'll save you time, get you a better price, and get you the right policy. Some of the questions that they might ask you are things like:

- Have you implemented multi-factor authentication, and is it fully enforced?

- How often are you doing backups, and are you making sure that they're separate from the rest of your network?

- What kind of firewall do you use, and is it up-to-date and properly configured?

- What type of endpoint protections do you have in place?

- Can you prove that the endpoint protections are running on every device?

- Do you have a true incident response plan, and have you tested it with a tabletop exercise?

- How do you manage access permissions?

- How do you provoke access permissions when an employee leaves your company?

- Do you regularly perform penetration tests?

- Do you have a data loss prevention mechanism in place to protect your data so that if somebody emails something out by mistake, it stops before it gets out of your network?

Let's take a look back at pre-existing conditions. Recently, there was a lawsuit in which the folks at Travelers, one of the largest insurance companies in the United States, took an organization to court because they didn't have all the things that they committed to having in place. Travelers didn't just deny the claim; they're actually suing the organization itself, because this organization claimed that they had multi-factor authentication in place, and Travelers found out that they didn't after the organization was hit with a ransomware attack. They decided that it would be much more prudent to take the organization to court and argue the misrepresentation influenced their risk acceptance in this situation. Now do you think that this victim thought that they had everything in line for their cyber insurance? Of course they did. The problem originated when somebody on their team was filling out something called a self-assessment questionnaire (SAQ) and answered the question regarding Multi-factor Authentication incorrectly. This is something that your insurance provider provides to you to identify what types of controls you have in place to help reduce the risk. Unfortunately, in this situation, we're talking about fraud. The intention might not have been to commit fraud, but that's where Travelers took the case.

What if this happened to your firm? You didn't intend to commit fraud, but now one oversight on your SAQ and your firm is being called fraudulent. Do you know what happens when you try to get new cyber insurance in that scenario, or when a partner or a vendor finds out? You should ask who is filling out your security self-assessment questionnaires at your firm. Most of these self-assessment questionnaires are being filled out by managing partners or people who really don't know what is happening in the control side of their network. That's a big problem. If an incident happens, the cyber insurer isn't going to accept excuses. Self-reporting is over.

It would be bad to be rejected by an insurer before you get a policy, but it's far worse to think that you have coverage and then to have your claim rejected when you need it the most. Don't go it alone. This seems like a heavy lift, but there's an answer that makes it easier for you. Consider having a third party come in and do an assessment.

Find out all of your vulnerabilities now, proactively. You could get peace of mind right now by knowing that you're either protected properly, or where the risks lie that you need to address. Don't wait for that cyber insurance renewal to come up. If you're interested in getting a complimentary cybersecurity assessment, go to **csoscott.com/analysis** and schedule your 15-minute discovery call with me. You'll gain peace of mind, and get the most important items knocked out before you try to get your cyber insurance renewed or modified.

Chapter 12:

Picking the Right Cybersecurity Solutions

In this chapter, I'm going to cover what I believe is a very important topic: five ways to make sure that your firm isn't wasting money on the wrong cybersecurity tools, and how to actually know and verify that what you have is working.

In 2015, IBM made a simple prediction. They predicted that cybercrime would become the number one issue for every company on earth. Recently, trends have suggested that by the end of 2025, damages from cybersecurity criminals will be in the trillions of dollars. If you do the math, that means that every minute, $900 million is spent in recovery and damages from cybercrime events. It's already the number one issue. That makes your cybersecurity provider a major player in the success of your firm. Some IT companies even provide cybersecurity services, which is very common. However, can they help you become secure enough to help you get insurance, survive a claim, and most importantly, recover?

Not all IT companies are created equal. We work with a third party that goes through and does IT audits for providers, and they shared a little bit of information with me that I thought was really interesting. Over the last six months, less than half of the networks they audited would be able to successfully make a cyber insurance claim, because their cybersecurity policies and procedures were so bad. The worst part of the story is that most of these companies actually provided cybersecurity services themselves. So, not all cybersecurity companies are created equal, either.

When you're looking at a cybersecurity company, there's a couple of things that you should consider. First, you should think about what they are going to provide for your organization. An effective cybersecurity company should reduce the risk of cyber-attacks. They should help you protect networks from unauthorized exploitation. They should help you create an incident response plan that will reflect against disruption of services. Also, they should help your firm meet industry and cyber insurance standards.

Many of you reading this are facing the FTC regulations that kicked in June of 2023. These new regulations carry some massive fines. In this chapter, I'm going to go through five simple steps for picking the right cybersecurity provider.

First, we're going to go through and talk about getting clear about what cybersecurity really means to your firm. Then we're going to go through and spend a little bit of time getting everyone on the same page about the right questions you need to ask when you're interviewing a cybersecurity company. We're going to talk about checking a provider's reputation, and ultimately, clarify what they offer and how it relates to your firm.

The first thing is getting clear on how your firm defines cybersecurity. It's not about going through and buying all the tools that you can afford. Buying a bunch of security tools will not protect your firm. Unless you know what to buy, you could actually be wasting money and still end up at risk. Your firm needs the right tools and ultimately the right strategy for your specific organization. You wouldn't just walk into a pharmacy if you were feeling sick and go through and buy every item on the shelf, right? Instead, you would contact your doctor, make an appointment, and you would discuss the appropriate options. Your doctor would ask some questions to understand your health risks and what's going on. Next, your doctor may take a blood sample or do other tests to determine the best course of action. After sending that sample or test to an independent lab, your doctor would prescribe a prescription or treatment plan, with specific guidelines. That's what you do to help mitigate health risks and to address issues when you're not feeling well. Shouldn't you do the same thing when it comes to your cybersecurity?

It's not about the size of your organization. About six months ago, we had a small law firm that had just two people in it that got hit by ransomware. Attackers broke in after the firm downloaded a fake QuickBooks payroll update by mistake. The hackers were able to get into their QuickBooks system, and from there were able to get onto each device. Then they were able to go through and monitor the small law firm's behavior. After that, they were able to hold all of their data ransom.

They did this a couple of ways. The first is that they had locked everything down, making it impossible for the small law firm to access any of their data out of the network. Then they used that data to move on and phish other victims, all the while extorting the exact amount of money the small law firm happened to have in their bank account. This is happening and it doesn't matter about the size of your firm or your organization. In fact, small firms are low-hanging fruit, because you have the fewest tools.

Your cybersecurity prescription should have things like safety, compliance, and recovery. On the safety side, you need a strong security stack of different solutions that have a little bit of strategic overlap built into them to keep your organization safe. Does your provider keep this entire stack updated regularly? On the compliance side of things, think about FTC safeguards. Does the cyber security company understand what requirements your firm faces with these new strict regulations? On the recovery side, can they help you address any incident quickly and efficiently?

If your health was on the line, you wouldn't just go to any doctor. As much as we all love our family doctor, if you had a serious condition, you would go to a specialist, right? The same is true when it comes to your firm's cybersecurity. You don't want to just go to anyone providing cybersecurity. When something as important as your firm is on the line, you need to go to a cybersecurity specialist. The right cybersecurity advisor or your firm will know these different requirements. This is a big reason that the California Lawyers Association, the Society of California, and countless other associations have come to us as their cybersecurity partner to protect their members. Cybersecurity is all we live, breathe, and do.

A virtual chief security officer can also fill that role at your firm. This is someone who focuses on cybersecurity, understands your firm, and knows the cyber threat landscape specific to firms. This is so important because your firm has specific requirements. Furthermore, your industry has specific requirements, as I've already mentioned with FTC safeguards. There are going to be some specific rules and regulations that may apply to your firm, depending on the size. Some of this is based on things like your geographical location. Others might be based on commitments your firm makes for cyber insurance. The right cyber security advisor for your firm is going to know all of this.

The second big thing is getting everyone on board. The right advisor will get everybody on board. Ultimately, cybersecurity is a team effort that needs to start from the head down. Choosing and working with the right solution involves everyone in your organization.

Think about the event MGM recently had. One simple phone call cost hundreds of millions of dollars. You know that MGM had invested in the right tools to protect their casinos, but it all came down to a single employee's mistake.

When it comes to cybersecurity, everyone matters. It's not just "something that the IT people can deal with", as so many people think. The executives need to be a part of the conversation. Ultimately, employees at all levels need to be trained. The cybersecurity provider you choose will need to work with everyone.

The third thing that I want to talk about is asking the right questions when you're choosing that cybersecurity provider. Some important questions include:

- What makes you qualified to provide cybersecurity for my firm?
- How accessible are you?
- Are you insured?
- Do you understand how a firm operates?
- What can you do for my firm if something goes wrong?

- How well do you communicate with your clients?
- What methods do you use?
- How will you assess the needs of firms?
- What steps will you take?
- What steps do you take for your own cybersecurity?
- What makes you qualified to provide firm cybersecurity services?

What you're looking for here is whether they have experience with firms specifically. You're also looking for certifications, an advanced cybersecurity stack, and expertise on the FTC and other compliances your firm needs to be aware of and navigate.

You also need to make sure that they are easily accessible, especially for emergencies. You want to make sure that they have regular office hours, and that they have some sort of after-hours availability. Think about your doctor again. If you're having an emergency, you want to make sure that you can reach out to them. Ultimately, you will want to make sure that you can reach them easily via phone or email.

The next question is, are they insured? Do they have an errors and omissions policy? Are they able to provide you with a certificate of coverage? The right vendor is an insured vendor. Not only do they need to be insured, but they should be insured specifically for the things that your firm needs protection from.

The right provider is also going to be familiar with the operations inside of a firm. They'll know the best ways to keep you safe without disturbing any of your daily work. You also need to know what they will do for your firm if something goes wrong. The right provider can help you do things like create an annual update for your incident response plan.

Another important question is how do they communicate with their clients? The right provider can relay complex security issues clearly in plain language that you can understand. The right provider can also keep you updated on changes in the cyber landscape, effectively and efficiently as they arise.

Speaking of communication, a critical component is after-hours events. Hackers aren't working 9 to 5. An effective provider is going to respond to your questions quickly, and is ready to go when there's an event. You may want to review their technical support to see if they actually have some sort of 24/7 coverage, which is key for most firms. An effective cybersecurity provider can also offer a human on the other end of the phone when you call their office. When you call their office, somebody should actually pick up the phone and help you instead of saying, "For your convenience, go to our website for support."

An effective provider can also keep clients informed of changes that are happening in the cybersecurity landscape. This might be a question you ask when you do reference checks for this provider. When was the last time your existing provider did a quarterly technology business review to cover the latest threats on how your network is set up effectively and on how they're protecting you?

Another question is, how will the provider assess the needs of your firm? An effective provider is a good listener. They make use of third-party assessments, and apply their understanding of your firm and your industry to create great cybersecurity solutions that allow you to invest in protecting yourself from the highest risk items.

Next, you should find out what steps they take for their own cyber security. When you're looking for that right provider, it's best to find one that has a third-party to review their own security. You'll want to find one that keeps up to date on current and new threats. You'll also want to make sure to find one that has updated cybersecurity insurance.

The next thing that we want to talk about is checking the provider's reputation. Your cybersecurity provider should have a proven track record in your market. They should be already working with a number of firms. You might want to find out if they have industry recognition. Look for simple things like affiliations: are they part of the same association that you are? You can also ask for references to understand how other firms have had success with this provider.

Also, you can assess their focus on innovation by reviewing their history. Are they enhancing their offerings and expanding their portfolio to address all of the changes that are happening inside the cybersecurity landscape constantly? It's said that one of the big truths with cybersecurity is that it's a constantly-moving target. What we did yesterday is no longer effective tomorrow.

Finally, you'll want to make sure to clarify what the provider offers. Do they offer elements that support your firm being compliant, especially with FTC regulations? Ask them how they handle incident recovery. Do they help you with your plan? Do they have their own written plan? You'd be surprised how often this is not in your general MSP's wheelhouse. The majority of MSP's are generalists. Cybersecurity is too important and specialized, which is why you really want somebody that is a professional expert in that arena.

Being able to quickly recover might be the difference between life and death for your firm. The right provider is going to guide you through that process. What do they offer? Does what they offer coincide with the risks inside of your firm? An effective cybersecurity provider can offer you a number of things. They should offer you a strategy, they should offer you a prescription, and they should offer you security and compliance. Ultimately, they become your trusted cybersecurity doctor, a trusted advisor.

I know that you're concerned about the price, but cyber security is not about bargain shopping. Price is an ineffective guide for selecting a trusted cyber security advisor. Think about it this way. If you had been exposed to a dangerous toxin, and needed to know if any damage had been done or if there were further actions needed for your health, would you be looking for the cheapest doctor? Never use the lowest price as your determining factor; and by the same token, never use the highest. It ultimately comes down to trust. Who do you have the most confidence in? Who is going to be able to do the job effectively? Remember that a lower price might mean fewer services, less security, lower quality, and no trusted advisor. This means no one you can turn to when you have an issue or question, and no one who knows the strategy in your organization to help reduce your risk. You could even find yourself on your own during an event.

How does this happen? As I touched on earlier, this can happen when the provider offers IT, but they're not a cybersecurity expert. Security is only an add-on to them, it's not a hyper-focus. Sure, they can offer a tool, but do they really have an effective plan that meets your firm's needs? Think of it this way: a lab technician works in a hospital, but they aren't qualified to give you a proper physical.

I know it's easier to just look at the price. Theoretically, yes, you could go with the bargain basement option. Before you do that, though, just consider a few facts. The average cost of a data breach is $3.9 million. Why are these so expensive? The answer is, Hackers know that breaches can determine your relationship with clients. They know they have the power and potential to destroy these relationships. They know they stop your firm's production. Ultimately, these threaten the financial security of everyone around you. Think of that small law firm I mentioned earlier in the chapter. The hackers emailed every one of their clients. Can you imagine every one of your clients at your firm getting an email from you with a link in it? Would they click it? Quite possibly.

Studies have found that 28% of small businesses that were hit by a data breach last year, (PR Newswire, 2019). 25% of those small businesses declared bankruptcy after the cyber event, and 10% of those actually went out of business altogether after the breach (PR Newswire, 2019). In the end, the right provider is about protecting your firm, data, your reputation, and your future.

So, what's the best way to get started? Just like with a doctor, you start with a simple checkup, or in this case, a cybersecurity risk assessment. You can schedule a simple checkup where a cybersecurity expert can ask you a few questions and learn about your firm's current risks. They'll work to understand what matters to you, figure out how your current tools are stacking up, and determine what's working and what's not.

In fact, with the FTC regulations and serious fines impacting every single firm in the United States, an assessment is one of the key requirements every firm needs to have completed at least one done per year. The best practice, for your own sake, is to have them done quarterly. There are two major factors that firms in the United States are facing, especially with the new FTC regulations. One is the strict compliance requirements, and the other is actually keeping your firm secure.

Being compliant doesn't necessarily mean being secure. That's why I highlight the fact that the FTC and your cybersecurity insurance policies now require you to have one of these assessments done once per year. I recommend that you have these done quarterly, because so many changes are made on your network, there's constantly things that need to be updated.

Chapter 13:

Stopping Social Engineering Before it Stops YOU

In this chapter, stopping social engineering before it stops you and your company. I'm going to go through five steps to increase your firm's safety.

Let's begin with an example. The MGM Grand is a name synonymous with entertainment. It's a name synonymous with winning. It's a name that comes up when you think about great places to go. It's also now the name of one of the biggest ransomware attacks in history using social engineering, and it only took one phone call. MGM reported being impacted for 10 days. According to a number of different sources, each one of those days cost them $8.4 million. Did they have cyber security? Of course they did. They're one of the biggest Casinos in the United States. They had some of the best security in the world. Did they have a full time dedicated team? Yes, absolutely. They're a casino. They invest in their people. Did they understand the importance of rules? Yes, casinos have teams of people who are great at following the rules. So, what happened?

It all boils down to simple human error. Did you know that up to 90% of malicious data breaches involve some sort of social engineering *(Firewall Times, 2023)*? Did you know that 75% of cyber-attacks and cyber threats to organizations involve social engineering *(Nguyen & Bhatia, 2020)*?

What is social engineering? According to Microsoft, it's simply going through and manipulating human behavior and error in order to gain access to sensitive or confidential information. Social engineers convince their victims to willingly hand over requested information like usernames and passwords. It also gets them to go even further and do things like let the attacker into the environment. A lot of this comes down to psychological manipulation like instilling fear, creating a false sense of urgency, appealing to greed or curiosity, establishing authority, building rapport, and exploiting social norms. It exploits human behavior and beliefs.

For example, take the castle and moat belief. People assume that if you can get past the moat, you belong in the castle. That means if someone can get past the receptionist, for example, then employees assume that person belongs in the office. Therefore, they are more likely to share company info with that person.

There are five things that you need to know about this:

1. 45% of employees click emails they consider to be suspicious, just in case it's important *(The Security Company, 2022)*.

2. On average, social engineering attacks cost about $4.76 million *(IBM, 2023)*.

3. 45% of employees don't report suspicious messages, out of fear of getting in trouble *(Dark Reading, 2020)*.

4. The costliest social engineering cyber attack is business email compromise. It's 64 times worse than ransomware at this point *(Polymer, 2022)*.

5. Social engineering doesn't just deploy ransomware, or go through and access somebody's email. It uses your firm's time, productivity, and it also impacts your reputation.

So, why do hackers use it so much? Because it works. There are different types of social engineering, including phishing, spear phishing, baiting, waterholing, vishing, smishing, pretexting, and quid pro quo. Let's take a closer look at each one of these.

First, let's focus on phishing. This is the most common type of social engineering. Basically, an attacker steals confidential information or company information through emails, voicemails, instant message, online ads, or even fake websites. Phishing can be successful because the fake information or deception looks highly authentic. Also, phishing makes victims feel a false sense of urgency, fear, or curiosity. This directs their focus on the fabricated information for a short period of time, so that they become too preoccupied to determine the authenticity of the information itself. Phishing is like a big net trying to get as many people as possible.

There's also a more sophisticated methodology. This is called spear phishing. It's more targeted than phishing. It focuses on specific victims, such as enterprise executives or network administrators. This allows them to customize highly effective phishing schemes based on the characteristics, positions, contacts, and other information about the victims.

Along with spear phishing comes baiting. This exploits people's desire for rewards, and lures them into a trap. While this approach is similar to phishing in many aspects, baiting emphasizes benefits that trap the victims. Actors only need to design something that looks attractive, such as links to websites that promise free gifts or links to attractive activities. One way that baiting can be very successful is getting people to think that they've won a trip somewhere.

Waterholing, on the other hand, is basically a method that attackers use to identify the websites frequently accessed by specific groups, like IT administrators. They then deploy malicious programs on those websites. When the victims access the websites, their computers become infected.

There's also vishing, which is based on phone calls. In these forms of attacks, the attacker tricks somebody into doing something based on a telephone call. Attackers set up entire call centers in order to make this possible. Smishing, on the other hand, uses SMS messages to engage their victims. These two approaches are clearly aimed at elderly victims who are not as familiar with the Internet, or don't know about this type of trick.

Quishing is a technique where attackers create malicious QR codes to steal sensitive information. In this attack, a user scans a QR code thinking it's from a trusted source, and is redirected to a malicious website. Once on this malicious website, the victim could be prompted to download malware.

There are more high-tech attacks that are also used when it comes to text messaging and voicemails. Pretexting, where attackers assume a false identity of an authority figure, such as law enforcement or maybe even somebody in your organization to deceive victims. The attacker usually disguises themselves as a person in authority to compel the victims to provide important information as instructed. As an example, the attacker might pose as a county official trying to resolve a parking ticket issue, and requires the victim to provide additional information like social security number or driver's license ID.

Quid pro quo relies on a different type of technique. It relies on the exchange of information or services to make the victims cooperate in giving out their important personal information. An example might be an attacker pretends to be IT calling about an upgrade, and requests login information to complete the process.

The whole process of social engineering is pretty straight forward. It starts with the preparation phase, and then it moves to the penetration phase. The difference between the preparation phase and the penetration phase is that in the preparation phase, they're basically going through and gathering information, setting up different systems that they're going to use in order to get into that environment. In the next phase, that's when the attack on the victim finally begins. Once the hacker has had enough, there's usually some sort of withdrawal situation.

In the preparation phase, attackers prepare by collecting the background information of the victims. In this phase the attack mainly focuses on identifying the victims and determining the best approach in launching social engineering attacks.

Next, we have the penetration phase. This is where attackers initiate contact with the victim. At the attack phase, the attackers begin collecting target data of the victim using different tools. This may be the information obtained to launch new attacks.

Finally, there's the withdrawal phase. This is after they've achieved their goals and the attackers are trying to erase all tracks of their illicit activities. In some cases, the victims won't be aware that the attack occurred. However, in most cases these days, this is where ransomware ends up getting deployed.

So, how do you protect your firm? There are 5 simple steps that I want to go through with you here:

- Educate and train your staff.
- Make sure you implement strong authentication practices.
- Create a culture of security.
- Obtain regular assessments.
- Develop an incident response plan.

Let's go through each of these, starting with educating your team. Be prepared for social engineering and, more importantly, avoid being tricked yourselves. Make sure your team is aware of human-induced attacks and human risks. There are some tools and websites that can be used to simulate social engineering attacks to hone the person's anti-fraud capabilities. You can also publicize real-world cases to deepen their impressions, especially cases involving close relationships such as colleagues or friends. This is going to make people feel that this is not a distant possibility, but a very real one. It also helps your team understand that it's okay for them to bring up something that's going on in the environment.

The next step is to implement strong authentication protocols. When someone accesses your system, they should have to prove that they are who they say they are. That's where authentication comes in. It involves presenting credentials or evidence of identity, which are then verified against pre-established criteria. Common authentication factors include things like knowledge-based factors. This could be passwords, PIN numbers, or security questions. Another form of authentication factor is possession-based factors. These could be things like smart code, security tokens, or mobile devices. This could also include biometric factors, things like fingerprints, facial recognition, or iris scans. There are also location-based factors that can be used to identify somebody based on their geological location and geological data.

You're probably familiar with multi-factor authentication. This is a good example of a strong authentication method. Instead of just using one of the different factors that I mentioned earlier, you're using at least two of them. While MFA may not be required for your firm, multi-factor authentication is required for things like cyber insurance. This is because having multi-factor authentication creates an extra layer of identity. There have been a couple of insurance claims that were denied because of lack of multi-factor authentication. That makes it a vital part of any cyber security plan.

This reminds me of a very important story. In fact, this example is probably one of the most important in recent times, since it set precedence in a very scary way. There was a firm that had a breach recently. They filed a claim with their insurance company Travelers, one of the largest. As it turned out, during the investigation, the firm had falsely or incorrectly filled out their cyber insurance application, claiming that they had multi-factor authentication when they didn't. Travelers could have just denied the claim, which is common practice, leaving the firm with no coverage, which is bad enough. However, Travelers took the unprecedented step of filing for fraud and a lawsuit against this firm. Insurance companies base their risk-taking on these important factors. Too often we see applications that are filled out incorrectly. Since this incident, Travelers helped set a serious precedent with some major consequences.

The next step is to create a culture of security. Creating a culture of cybersecurity within an organization involves fostering a collective awareness and commitment to safeguarding digital assets and sensitive information. It begins with top-down leadership support, where executives prioritize and communicate the importance of cybersecurity. It also includes regular and engaging cybersecurity training programs for all employees. These play a critical part in building awareness and empowering individuals to recognize and respond to potential threats. I recommend you encourage open communication and non-punitive reporting, so that you can come up with a culture where your team is detecting security incidents early.

Implementing strong user-friendly security practices, coupled with regular updates and reminders, reinforces the importance of adherence to security protocols.

The next step is to obtain regular third-party assessments. Having a third-party assessment brings objectivity, expertise, and a comprehensive perspective to any firm's cybersecurity. These types of assessments can help your firm identify and address vulnerabilities, maintain compliance, and continuously improve your security posture. The benefits of a third-party assessment include compliance, risk mitigation, protecting your reputation, and reducing potential breaches.

The last step is to develop an incident response plan. An incident response plan is the key to recovery. A well-written incident response plan is a document that is formally approved by the senior leadership team, helps your firm educate and prepare team members for the event, divide up duties, and clarify roles during the incident response itself. It also minimizes potential damage and downtime.

Regular testing and updating of your firm's incident response plan is essential to ensure its effectiveness in the face of our evolving cyber threats today. The bottom line is, social engineering is dangerous and complex, and if you don't take these steps now, you're going to be dealing with a much more devastating impact later. Its danger and complexity lies in the fact that it's not a tech-based problem. It's a people-based problem.

Are you ready to protect your firm? My recommendation is you start where you're at today. We have a downloadable checklist to help you. Just go to **shielditnetworks.com** and get a free checklist we have available for social engineering. Your next step is to get a cybersecurity analysis done on your network. We're going to analyze your security, we'll meet with you and review the results, and we'll give you simple steps that you're going to be able to take to protect yourself and your firm's data.

Made in the USA
Columbia, SC
25 February 2025

4c6a1844-2982-4c94-850a-08527f86bd9dR01